Henry Houlding

Rhymes and Dreams

Legends of Pendle Forest and Other Poems

Henry Houlding

Rhymes and Dreams
Legends of Pendle Forest and Other Poems

ISBN/EAN: 9783337006495

Printed in Europe, USA, Canada, Australia, Japan

Cover: Foto ©Thomas Meinert / pixelio.de

More available books at **www.hansebooks.com**

Rhymes and Dreams,

Legends of Pendle Forest,

And other Poems.

BY

HENRY HOULDING.

"Rude rhymes, the which a rustic Muse did weave
In savage soil, far from Parnasso Mount,
And roughly wrought in an unlearned loom."
— *Spenser.*

BURNLEY:
Published by B. Moore, for the Joint Committee of the Literary and Scientific Club and the Literary and Philosophical Society.
MDCCCXCV.

PRELIMINARY NOTE.

MANY of our poets have lived amidst, and been inspired by, scenes of grandeur or of historic interest, to which our town can lay few claims. We have no mighty mountains forever uplifting their snow-clad peaks above the clouds. The surge and roar of the "ancient sea" falls not upon our inland ears. We have no great river bearing upon its tides richly laden Argosies from strange and far-off lands. Elsewhere have the great events of our national history been played out. Some faint echoes do reach our ears from the dim past, it is true, and it is also true that we have our Pendle Hill, our Boulsworth, our Hambledon, our moorland heights, at the feet of which nestle many a lonely dell or flowery glade. But these have found no place in the wandering artist's portfolio, and we have the happiness to possess no "Guide Book." But that our hills, and streams and valleys, and the common experiences of our workday life can inspire love and the beautiful expression of high and tender thoughts, this volume will abundantly prove. In the belief that what Mr. Houlding has written is worthy of a foremost place in our local literature, the Committee send forth this edition of his poems, confident that Burnley men at home and abroad will prize the work of one

"Who has found love in huts where poor men lie,
Whose daily teachers have been woods and rills,
The silence that is in the starry sky,
The sleep that is among the lonely hills."

THE COMMITTEE.

CONTENTS.

	PAGE
PREFACE	ix

RHYMES AND DREAMS.

TIMES AND FLOWERS	3
SUMMER SKIES	5
BY THE RIVER	8
AUTUMN LEAVES	11
IN A STONY DELVE	13
THE SONG OF BRUN	17
A FOREST DREAM	25
THE SNOW-SPIRITS (EXTWISTLE MOOR)	29
IN THE WOOD	33
KNOTGRASS	36
A DARK DAY (NETHERWOOD)	39
PRIMROSES	41
MEETING STREAMS	44
UNDER THE SNOW	46
FORGETFULNESS	50
SUNRISE	53
SUMMER DAYS	55
CHANGE	57
HAUNTED	58
SHADOWS	60
NIGHT COMETH	61
AN UNKNOWN BOURNE	63

NIGHTSHADE	64
WHITHER	66
A STILL SMALL VOICE	67
BY WAYS UNKNOWN	69
EDEN	71
A LONELY RIVER	72
VIATICUM	73
INWARD LIGHT	74
THE KING'S GARDEN	77
ASPHODELS	79

RHYMES AND DAYS.

CHILDHOOD	85
BOYHOOD	86
FRIENDSHIP	87
ASPIRATION	88
EVENSONG	89
AFTER MANY YEARS	90
A PORTRAIT	91
THE LOST PILGRIM	92
THE DEAD YEARS	93
FOREBODINGS	94
ACCUSATION	95
HUMILITY	96
AN OLD BOOK	97
MY GARDEN	98
WASTE PLACES	99
A STAR	100
BROTHER AND SISTER	101
HEAVENLY LOVE	102
COMPENSATION	103
BEREAVEMENT	104
REGRETS	105

CONTENTS.

WAITING	106
VISION	107
REALITY	108
EVANGELIST	109
YORICK	111
ORSINI	113
AT HURSTWOOD	114
A KEEPSAKE	115
FORGETMENOT	118
EVENING SHADOWS	119
THE TWO SPIRITS	120
A NIGHT-WATCH	121
A SONG OF REST	123
A SONG OF HEROES	125
LULLABY	129
PÆAN	132
A MIGHT-HAVE-BEEN	134
'T WAS SUNSHINE STILL WITH THEE	135
THE LOCKET	138
A DREAM OF THE PAST	139
THE TRUMPETS ARE SOUNDING	140
A REQUIEM	142
A MEETING	145
BENISON	147
BOON	147
AT REST	148
IF I REMEMBER	150
CLEOPATRA	152
A QUESTION OF IMMORTALITY	154
LOCH ACHRAY	155
DALMALLY	158
A TRUE FORGETMENOT	160

CONTENTS.

A QUARTETTE	162
A BIRTHDAY RHYME	164
ON A CERTAIN POEM	166
A SILVER WEDDING	170
A MEMORY	172
A CENOTAPH	176
A RHYME OF JUBILEE	184
FOR A "PENNY READING"	193
EPILOGUE	196
PROLOGUE	201
FOR A HOUSE OF HEALING	206

ESSAYS IN BLANK VERSE.

FAIRY FANCIES	217
MOONRISE	222
INVOCATION	224
THE RIDGE OF SNOW	226
A WALK TO RED LEES	229

LEGENDS OF PENDLE FOREST.

MALKIN TOWER	237
FRIAR DORIEN	251
THE WHITE WITCH	260
THE WEIRD WOMAN	290

FRAGMENTS.

DARK MORNINGS	313
THE MOON	314
GREETINGS	316
ADMER: A MYSTERY	317
NOTES	321

PREFACE.

I have been asked to give some account of these dreams.

But it is not easy to render an account of one's dreams to those who have no dreams of their own, or to those whose dreams are of a different tribe and kindred. I have already given some reminiscences of the conditions of life in Burnley fifty years ago, and of that sweeter life of nature that lies so close to it, and which compensates us for much of its ugliness and squalor, in two papers which I read some years ago before the members of the Literary and Scientific Club, and which are printed in the Society's Transactions, under the title of "Local Glimpses." I must refer the curious to these essays as some help to the interpretation of such of the pieces contained in this volume, as seem to need any. Something, however, I may say here, briefly, as becomes a preface.

This little volume is the outcome of much solitary communion with nature, and of much reading of very few books. My intercourse with nature has been limited in its range, by the hills that surround Burnley, to a few haunting rambles in the valleys of the Brun, the Calder and Pendle Water, and a few holiday excursions to the ridges and among the recesses of the moors. It is there I have come face to face with nature—its beauty and mystery—and having once seen that, we shall see no more, though we wander the wide world over. My reading has been as limited. Much reading of many books is only for those who have much leisure. For those whose time and opportunities are absorbed in "the busy street and the narrow life," much reading of very few books may serve as well. With Shakespeare for his friend and companion, one may "know more of man" than all the books of philosophy can tell us; with Wordsworth and Emerson for his daily teachers, one may see more of nature from his own back-door, than another who has travelled over the Alps and seen the sun rise over the islands of the "utmost sea." I cannot speak at length here of these books of mine, but they have had much to do with my dreams; and though they don't explain, they in some measure account for them. I had learnt something of the same lesson from other books. There were voices crying in the wilderness before the great voices could be heard clearly above the rest—poets, critics, preparers of the way; Hazlitt, Coleridge, Shelley, Leigh Hunt—my "Evangelist" of forty years ago. These led the way to Wordsworth, and Wordsworth to Emerson. I learnt from Wordsworth that the beauty we see in nature we "half create," that there is in nature

> "A presence that disturbs us with the joy
> Of elevated thoughts; a sense sublime
> Of something far more deeply interfused."

And this thought is more than echoed by Emerson in such passages as these:—"The beauty of these fair objects is imported into them from a metaphysical and eternal spring." "The mind is part of the nature of things." "The spirit that suffices quiet hearts, that seems to come forth to such from every dry knoll of sere grass, from every pine-stump and half-imbedded stone, on which the dull March sun shines, comes forth to the poor and hungry, and such as are of simple taste." "We exaggerate the praises of local scenery. In every landscape the point of astonishment is the meeting of the sky and the earth. The stars at night look down on the brownest, homeliest common with all the spiritual magnificence which they shed on the Campagna, or on the marble deserts of Egypt."

There is no "exaggeration of local scenery" in this book, no set descriptions. Nature is not "scenery;" it is something ideal and divine. But I may say a word or two about my old walks and Burnley's "ancient neighbourhood," for it is also written that "the mind loves its old home."

Fifty years ago, Towneley Park, as we called it, was feathered down to the old lodge with pines and sycamores, with woods of "oak, and elm and the bonny birch tree." "Meeting hazels darkened" over the stream, whose banks were not walled in as they are now, and the road went right away past clumps and avenues of great trees, past the hall, through Causey-end Wood, and out at the gate where the great oak stands that has stood there for so many centuries. There was a wood, in those days, on the Bacup Road, above Easden Clough—a mile-long avenue of larch trees, where the wild birds sang, and the wind chanted its eternal litanies; and where that "happiest of men," of whom Emerson speaks, who has "learnt from nature the lesson of worship," might have walked as in cathedral aisles. Burnley Wood was a country hamlet. Moseley Hill was further away than it is now. The sylvan approaches to Heasandford began at the old well near the "Brig o' Brown." Pendle stands where it did; but there was not the same smoke-cloud then between the village and the hill. We had not so many long streets to pass before we could see the dappled shadows of "that hill sublime." There were rural walks, where now there are railways. There were wells of pure water by the waysides, where the thirsty villagers could drink without peril of microbes. There was a beautiful waterfall overhung with bracken and brambles, where now there is a colliery. I see it in my dreams. I see the clear stream lapsing down over the rocks, among the mosses and ferns. I see the "midges" dancing over it in the shadow of the trees.

The composition of these poems covers, with wide intervals, a period of over forty years. Dates are appended to the two last sections, "Essays in Blank Verse" and "Legends of Pendle Forest." indicating the period at which the pieces were written. The poems in sonnet form at the beginning of "Rhymes and Days" and many other pieces of the same section belong to the same period. Others are of later date, as also are the poems in the first section. These "Rhymes and Dreams," as I have called them, are mainly occupied with one theme— the mystery of nature, and the beauty. They are not transcripts of scenery, but reflexes of the Vision, by which the wanderer in time is "on his way attended;" and of certain momentary glimpses that come to us,

"In vacant or in pensive mood,
 And flash upon that inward eye,
 Which is the bliss of solitude."

H. H.

POEMS.

RHYMES AND DREAMS.

The rounded world is fair to see,
Nine times folded in mystery.
—*Emerson.*

The outward shows of sky and earth,
Of hill and valley, he has viewed ;
And impulses of deeper birth
Have come to him in solitude.
—*Wordsworth.*

TIMES AND FLOWERS.

THE meadow was full of sunshine
   And blossoming cups of gold,
And the warm, sweet breath of summer flowers,
   When life was a summer old.

The valley was white with star-blooms
   And May-flowers pale and fair,
And the clouds were white in the azure noon,
   When a dreaming boy came there.

The blue vetch grew in the hedgerow,
   And wild briar blushed above,
When a youth walked into the greenwood
   And pulled him a rose for love.

Between the yellowing lindens
    The tree of darkness grew,
When a man came out of the bride-chamber
    And gathered him slips of yew.

The purple heather was fading
    On moorland ridges brown,
When an old man wandered across the fell,
    As the lingering day went down.

Untrodden in all the pathways,
    The flowers are left to die,
And the moon comes over the lonely hill,
    And a moaning wind goes by.

SUMMER SKIES.

"For the world was from the beginning beautiful."
—*Emerson*

EVERMORE a dream will haunt me,
   Under these resplendent skies,
Fitter to o'er-roof the angels,
Or the pure-lived deities,
Than these earthward-gazing mortals,
Caring for their lives of care,
Seldom with uplifted faces
Yearning for diviner air.
What care they for all the glories
Of the cloud-rack sunward driven,
For the sapphire portals opening
On the infinitudes of heaven?
Even those who, "with the vision
And the faculty divine,"
Seek to pierce the veiling splendour,

Seek the temple's inner shrine,
What behold they? What do children
Gazing on the flowers behold
Of the mystery that lurketh
'Neath the azure and the gold?
For they see as children only
That the earth is fair with flowers,
And the heavens are built divinely
By the good eternal powers.

Evermore the world is lovely,
With bright streams and shadowing woods,
Yellow fields and purple moorlands,
Where the silent spirit broods;
Lovely is the blue horizon,
And the ether soft and clear,
And the silver hills of cloudland,
And the white moon's wandering sphere;
Morning dawns in mists of amber,
Evening sets in seas of gold,
And the hollow dark revealeth
Night and all its glories old.
Such a house for gods to dwell in,
Builded high in space and time,
Ne'er was seen in prophet's vision,
Ne'er was sung in poet's rhyme.
And we walk about and wonder,

While the ages roll away
That shall foster nobler races,
Worthier of the night and day ;
Worthier to read the cypher,
Worthier to know the sign
That in flower and star proclaimeth
Earth is heaven, and heaven divine ;
In the fulness of the æons,
Worthier to realise,
Dreamer, more than all thou dreamest,
Under these ethereal skies !

BY THE RIVER.

I WALKED in a lonely place,
   Where ferns and mosses grow,
Where, with a wild and pendulous grace,
   The tall sedge droopeth low,
     Over the brim of the river.

I climbed the rugged wall
   Of rocks, so grey and old,
Where sits the sceptred hawkweed tall,
   With all its crowns of gold,
     Over the brim of the river.

I lay beneath the trees
   And heard the low winds sigh
For the far, forgotten centuries,
   Whose summer suns went by,
     Over the brim of the river.

I saw on either side
　　The cliffs shut in the scene,
And the evening clouds above them glide,
　　And the moon look down between,
　　　　Over the brim of the river.

I heard the cuckoo wake
　　The echoes of the hill ;
I heard the wild-bird in the brake
　　The woods with music fill,
　　　　Over the brim of the river.

I waited, till the moon
　　Grew brighter, and the air
Still, save for the mystic rune
　　The low wind murmured there,
　　　　Over the brim of the river ;

Save for the peaceful sound
　　Of the waters as they rolled,
Filling the vale above, around,
　　As it had done of old,
　　　　Over the brim of the river ;

I waited, till afar,
　So lonely and serene,
Looked large and bright the evening star,
　　Adown the dark ravine,
　　　　Over the brim of the river.

I waited, lingering still,
　In that enchanted dell,
And the thoughts that did my spirit fill
　My tongue can never tell,
　　　As I walked by the lonely river.

AUTUMN LEAVES.

I WALK where withered leaves are blown
  Beside the mountain stream, alone,
As once in happy days gone by—
So bright, so sweet, so swift to die—
I walked with one across whose dreams
Will come, perchance, far-wandering gleams
And murmurs from these northern streams;
In whose sweet voice there was a tone
Of rippling music like their own,
And in whose heart a sympathy
With nature's nameless mystery,
That like a brooding spirit dwells
By these lone streams and mountain dells
A sympathy too rarely found :
And now where withered leaves around
My feet by autumn winds are blown.

I walk, as I have walked, alone,
Thinking of all that I have known,
Of gentle natures, one or two,
Who knew the places that I knew,
Who lingered briefly as the flowers,
That leave us to the wintry hours
And leafless woods, where low winds sigh
Like voices of the years gone by;
Whose fallen leaves, yellow and grey,
Are trodden in the grass to-day,
To mingle, ere the linnet sings,
With dust of unremembered springs.

IN A STONY DELVE.

"And where the long street roars has been
The stillness of the central sea."
—Tennyson.

IN a stony delve outside the town
    I sat an hour ere the sun went down,
And I heard the wash of an ancient sea,
In a time long dead, o'er its sandy bed
Surge to and fro, to the music slow
Of winds and of tides that ebb and flow;
For so of old the rocks were laid,
In motion and music, in shimmer and shade,
And the moon came over the wave to see,
And the sun looked down rejoicingly,
And the stars were ablaze with jubilee,
When the solid frame of the hills was made.

And I saw of old how the stones were wrought,
How the sun, and the wind, and the waters brought
The living germ, how the lichen crept
On the barren ledge, and the mosses slept
In the morning mists of a thousand years :
While to and fro the waters go,
And day and night the soft winds blow,
Until the time of the flower appears,
And the time of the singing of birds in the tree :
And HE, on whose coming all creatures wait,
The tread of whose foot as he cometh late
Is felt on the shore of the lonely sea,
He cometh who is, and was to be,
The shaping hand and the voice of thought !

I sat in the delve as the sun went down,
And I heard the clink the hammers made,
When they builded the town of the sea-sand brown,
As the stones were wrought and the courses laid
Over the bed of the buried shore,
Where the tides of the sea had been before,
And the stones in the wall of houses tall
Heard the words of men in the street,
Heard the echoes of passing feet,
As friends, and lovers and neighbours meet,

Where the sea-bird once would come and go,
With the wash of the waters to and fro.

I sat in the delve as the sun went down,
Where the sea had left the sand-stone brown,
And a sound as of waves made symphony
With the sound of the words of men unknown,
With music of peace, and clamour of strife,
And voice of women and men who prayed,
Of prophets proclaiming eternal life,
And the silver laughter of boy and maid,
And songs of love, and songs of the soul,
And hymns and anthems that seemed to roll
Out of the depths of a DEEPER SEA,
Whose tides are the races of men to be,
On whose shores I seem to sit alone
And watch them coming by ways unknown,
Coming and going and seeking their own,
Lords of the sea, and lords of the land,
Of the vocal thought and the toiling hand.

And I saw in the delve of that ancient sea
How all that is or seemeth to be,
Is but for a time and passes away;
How man, too, cometh and must not stay;
And my soul was sad as I wandered down

IN A STONY DELVE.

In the twilight cold to my house in the town,
My house that is builded of sea-sand brown;
And a weird mist rose from the darkening stream
Under the wan moon's watery gleam,
And a moaning of winds came over the moor,
And the lights died out in the homes of the poor.

But in deep of night, when the winds were still,
And the crescent moon had gone over the hill,
I look'd up from the street, and the wonder sweet,
So new and so old, was revealed again,—
For the mist-cloud grey had melted away,
And over the roofs and the graves of men,
And over the delve of that ancient sea,
The stars were ablaze with jubilee!

ON THE BRUN.

Photo: Geo. Hy. Fields.

THE SONG OF BRUN.[1]

IN the time before the hills
    Heard the wandering hunter's horn,
Ere the valley had a name,
    Or the forest had a bourne.

When the wolf was on the fell
    And the fox was in the bush,
When the white moon woke the owl
    And the red dawn heard the thrush,

Heard the linnet in the tree
    On the bank above the pool,
Where the wren had made her nest
    Down among the mosses cool.

Then my little streamlet sang
    As it sings to me to-day,
To the wandering bee and bird
    Softly sang its roundelay.

Lonely for a thousand years,
   Through the brake the waters crept,
Singing in the lonely dell,
   Where the sylvan shadows slept;

Singing to the red-rose briar,
   Singing to the heathery scar,
Singing to the soaring lark,
   Singing to the evening star;

Singing to the wintry cloud,
   Singing to the summer noon,
Singing to the lonely night,
   Darkening o'er a crescent moon;

Singing to the wind that sang
   To the solitary tree,
With the singing wind it went
   Singing to the lonely sea.

In the hollow of the hills
   Went my merry moorland burn,
Talking all the summer through
   To the summer-scented fern,

To the slender sedges wild,
  To the nodding harebell blue,
To the bending willow-herb
  And the bending willow too;

Talking in the forest glade
  To the tall, red campion flower,
To the hawkweed, golden crowned,
  Buttressed on its rocky tower;

Whispering to the grassy fringe
  Of the white-flower-freckled lea,
Murmuring to the foxglove bells
  And the dim anemone.

So it went by heath and holme,
  Seeking still its kindred streams,
Like a wandering voice that goes
  Singing through a land of dreams;

Through a lone and happy clime
  To a lone and wondrous sea,
Singing as it sings to-day
  Of a wondrous mystery.

Summer birds of wandering wing
  Came to nestle in the trees;
Plumèd seeds from far-off wilds
  Floated down the autumn breeze;

Halcyons of azure mail
  From the willowy pools went by;
Herons flew from mountain meres
  Through the solitary sky:

Swallows skimmed the reedy marsh;
  Ravens swooped adown the gale;
Falcons from their kingly hills
  Skirted all the hollow vale.

All the nestling valley heard
  Sylvan music of the prime:
Heard the bell of noontide bee,
  And the beetle's drowsy chime;

Heard on summer's balmy winds
  Voices come and pass away,
Heard the lonely cuckoo bird
  Sing the song he sings to-day;

Heard the shrill-voiced ouzel-cock
    Piping in the bushes low ;
Heard the stock-dove's gentle coo
    On the soft wind come and go ;

Heard through all the lonely stream
    Sing its lonely mystery
Of a past and passing time,
    And a time that is to be :

Heard all these as one sole sound ;
    Heard all voices but the one,
For whose coming all the hills,
    Waiting, watch the patient sun :

Heard at last a voice that comes
    Through the vale to meet the morn ;
Heard a shout upon the hills ;
    Heard at last the hunter's horn !

Summer comes and summer goes,
    Winter goes to come again,
And a storm is on the hills,
    Thunder and the driving rain.

THE SONG OF BRUN.

Summer breezes from the south
    Come to meet the northern snows,
Storms of winter from the sea
    Come the way the west wind blows.

On the hills the driving rain,
    Through the glen the torrents sweep,
Bearing down their mountain spoil
    Roaring, moaning to the deep.

Roaring, moaning goes the burn,
    Moaning to the wintry noon,
Moaning to the lonely night
    Darkening o'er a crescent moon.

All night long the torrent moans
    Through the hollow vale forlorn,
Till with sunrise come again
    Echoes of a wandering horn !

Echoes come and pass away,
    Winding through the forest drear,
Sudden voices which the wolves
    In their ancient caverns hear ;

Savage voices of the chase
  Answer clear from scar to scar,
To the centuries of peace
  Heralding the years of war.

Mighty chieftains of the spear,
  Tribe with tribe at ruthless feud,
Slayers of the wolf are slain,
  By a fiercer foe subdued.

Chiefs of battle on the plain
  Lay at rest their mighty bones ;
Bearded priests with rites of blood
  Bring the fire and pile the stones.

Still the little moorland burn
  To the moorland bracken sings,
Where the buried ashes lie
  Of the old forgotten kings.

Sings its unforgotten song
  Of the old forgotten years,
When the mists of morning fled
  From the gleam of Roman spears !

Of a past and passing time,
  So the brown burn sings, and so
Will it sing, in time to come,
  To the men who come and go!

A FOREST DREAM.

SING soft and low, wild forest stream,
    Flow softly singing through my dream,
For in my dream the world is fair,
And in the golden summer air
Old Pendle lifts his ridge sublime,
A tower among the towers of time,
Lone looking through the ages drear
O'er many a path of ancient fear,
Where once an outcast gray and worn,
Came on his pilgrimage forlorn,
And there ascending took his stand
And saw a far celestial land.

Wild forest stream, I wander slow,
And in thy song, so sweet and low,
I hear far echoes of the prime,
Responsive, through the dream of time,
To prophet's prayer and poet's rhyme.

A FOREST DREAM.

Far-wandering from that summit grey
The dreaming prophet passed away,
As a cloud passes from the day :
Far-wandering, in as rapt a mood,
A bard of nature's solitude,
Who knew the mystery of the hills,
The power, the presence that fulfils
Lone places with a lonely light,
Far-looking knew the lonely height,
Steep rising over moorlands dun
Between him and the setting sun,
On Rylstone as he wandered slow
In visions of the Silver Doe,
What time a sound of gladsome power
From Bolton's old monastic tower
Rang wide around from fell to fell,
A wondrous tale the echoes tell,
And listening Pendle owns the spell.

A glory from the sun comes down,
Clothing that steep so bare and brown,
And time has crowned it with a crown ;
But over these a mystic gleam
Shines on me from the poet's dream,
And over these a light of God
Burns where that outcast's feet have trod.

Sing softly still, and gently flow,
Wild stream, beside thee as I go
In forest ways I seem to know,
Down to a river winding there,
Through sylvan valleys wide and fair,
And flowing westward to the sea
By homes of ancient mystery,
Lone, lovely, but of evil fame,
Where once a mighty minstrel came,
Masking awhile in shepherd's weed,
And piping on his oaten reed
To forest folk a forest rhyme,
Preluding to the golden time
When, with a wandering Redcross knight
And a king's daughter robed in white,
Undaunted by enchantments drear,
With song and silver harpings clear,
He journeyed from this wizard bourne
Far into "fairy lands forlorn."

Wild stream, thy song is soft and low,
Thy voice is with me as I go,
A voice that in the desert sings
The lonely mystery of things,
And in the blue and golden noon,
And the wan wonder of the moon,

And in the watches of the star,
Through the still forest weird and far,
Carols wild music of the prime,
A burden of the dawn of time,
A burden of the years untold,
The lapse of suns and summers old,
The fleeting glory on the hill,
The patient power abiding still,
And all the glamour and the gleam
Of things that be not what they seem,
And dreams that bards and prophets dream.

In the far forest, soft and low,
Wild stream, I hear thee singing so
A song the world will never know!

THE SNOW-SPIRITS.

(EXTWISTLE MOOR.)

THE snow has come in the cold, dim night,
　　Silently falling, so soft and white,
On the sleeping hills, and the frozen streams,
And the woods, at rest in their winter dreams.
Out of the cloud that came out of the sea
Cometh the beautiful mystery,
For the spirits that live in the upper air,
And fashion all shapes and marvels there,
The spirits of God that give us boon,
Awoke in the white mists under the moon,
And all night long, in the cold moonshine,
They moved unseen through the vapours fine,
Weaving a soft and silvery fleece
To cover the earth with comfort and peace;
For they know that a spirit is slumbering there,
Earth-born, but akin to the spirits of air,
That lieth adream through the wintry hours,
And nurseth the germs of the unborn flowers;

And out of the cloud, and out of the sea,
Moved by a wonderful sympathy,
They bring the soft and comforting snow
To cover the spirit that rests below.

And there in the churchyard dark and deep,
Where the nameless children of Lethe sleep,
Where, under the roots of the flowers, the mould
Is the dust of those who were loved of old ;
Softly and tenderly over the dead
A pure, white pall the spirits have spread,
And the air is hushed, as a mother mild
Hushes the song for her sleeping child,
Which she knows will awaken with bright clear
    eyes :
Do the spirits know that the dead will rise—
The spirits that live in the upper air—
That they cover the graves with such tender care?
Do they remember the nameless bones
That have lain for ages beneath the stones?
Do they pity and love, as they love the flowers
That will bloom again in the summer hours,
The hearts and faces whose hopes and tears
Have been buried and dead for a thousand years?
Do they know the mystery hidden there
Of death, that once was love and prayer ?

Did they hear, as they passed through the snow-
    cloud cold,
The prayers that ascended to heaven of old ?
Do they know the answer that none may know,
That they cherish the dust that lies below ?

Oh, fear not the spirits will do thee harm,
That work in the wintry clouds their charm :
Go boldly forth on the frozen hill
And up the valley, so silent and still ;
Go wander alone on the moorlands wild,
Where terrace on terrace the snow-heaps are
    piled ;
Go where the wind of the north may beat
Thy fever'd brow with its arrowy sleet;
If thou art wearied of life and its woe,
Go out on the homeless desert of snow,
And the spirits that live in the frozen air
Will come to thy spirit and comfort thee there,
As they comfort the flowers in their wintry nest,
As they comfort the dead in the graves that rest,
As they comfort the weary of heart and limb
Who drowsily swoon in snow-wastes dim,
While the frozen and feathery softness lies
Like a thin white dream on the frozen eyes !
As they comfort these they will comfort thee,
If with fearless footstep and spirit free,

THE SNOW-SPIRITS.

Thou goest alone on the bleak hill side,
And over the snow-lands trackless and wide,
Leaving behind thee the noise and strife
Of the busy street and the narrow life;
Not fearing nor hoping and having no care,
Asking not, seeking not, breathing no prayer,
Loving not anything here below,
But loving only the white, pure snow,
Full of wonder, and worship and laud,
For the miracle wrought by the angels of God,
The angels of beauty and mystery
That live in the clouds, that rise out of the sea :
Thus, if thou comest, and comest alone,
The spirits will know thee, and make thee their own,
Will know thee and love thee, and give thee a sign,
And the sense of an infinite peace shall be thine ;
And the trouble that wearies, the sorrow that kills,
Shall lie light on thy heart, as the snow on the hills !

IN THE WOOD.

IF it be true I cannot tell
   That spirits in the forest dwell, .
But walking in the wood to-day,
A vision fell across my way ;
Not such as once, beneath the green
O'er-hanging boughs, I should have seen ;
But in the tranquil noontide hour,
And in the crimson campion flower,
And in the grass I felt a power ;
And every leaf of herb and tree
Seemed like a voice that greeted me,
Saying, ' Not to ourselves alone
We live and die making no moan.
The sunshine and the summer showers,
And the soft dews of night are ours ;
We ask no more than what is given ;
Our praise and prayer is leaf and bloom,

And day and night our sweet perfume
Like incense rises up to heaven ;
Thus our sweet lives we live alone,
We come and go and make no moan.'

And so out of the wood I went,
Thinking, I too will be content
With day and night, with good and ill,
Submissive to the heavenly will ;
The power that gives to plant and tree
Its bound and limit, gave to me
Just so much love and so much life,
And whatsoever peace, or strife,
Or joy, or sorrow, may be mine,
Is bounded by a law divine.
I cannot do the things I would,
I cannot take the boundless good
Which love might bring or heart desire,
And though to heaven my thoughts aspire,
'T is only given me to behold,
Far off, its spheres of living gold.
The little orb on which I ride
Around the sun in circuit wide,
Is all an unknown land to me
And waters of an unknown sea.
The narrow bourne wherein I move,
This little world of hate and love,

Within whose set diurnal round
By strongest fate my feet are bound,
Has light upon it from afar,
As when a dungeon's iron bar
Crosses the splendour of a star.
This home of memory and care,
This cave of thought, this cell of prayer,
This House of Life in which I dwell,
Is vast as heaven and deep as hell,
And what it is I cannot tell.
Of this alone my mind is sure—
That in my place I must endure
To work and wait, and bide mine hour,
And take the sunshine and the shower;
Content to know the world is fair,
Though life is rooted fast in care;
To watch the far-off lights of heaven,
Yet ask no more than what is given;
Content to take what nature brings
Of all inexplicable things,
Content to know what I have known,
And live and die and make no moan.

KNOTGRASS.

> "And the dull swain
> Treads on it daily with his clouted shoon."
> —*Comus.*

I WANDER'D far o'er dale and down,
   By many a brave, historic town,
And many a home of old renown.

I went, from morn to eventide,
Through leafy lanes, and by the side
Of quiet farms and pastures wide;

By hedge-row elm and churchyard yew,
By poplars shooting to the blue,
By hills whereon the rock-rose grew;

By village-green and garden trim,
By river broad with sedgy brim,
By mossy bourne of woodlands dim.

Nine days I went with footsteps bold,
Through cities strange and kingdoms old,
From bourne to bourne, from wold to wold.

Nine days and nights, without a care,
I sought with wonder everywhere
If aught was strange, if aught was fair.

And one fair marvel that I found,
Under a bank with beeches crowned,
Was knotgrass covering all the ground.

Of all rare things I chanced to meet,
Was none so fresh, and strange and sweet,
As that green carpet to my feet.

Soft-pacing under leafy tent,
For half an endless hour I went
Along that pathway, "dew-besprent."

'T was worth the lonely leagues to see
That glimpse of sylvan mystery—
That little fringe of elfin lea,

Where, on the moonlight-hallowed green,
Night-tripping fays, in glimmering sheen
Of mystic pageantries, had been.

And this was far—so far away!
And now 't was but the other day
I found where thick the knotgrass lay,

As soft as that to walk upon,
As fit for court of Oberon,
And yet not half a league from Brun !

Twice five long years had passed, or more,
Since I had wandered kingdoms o'er,
To find what flourished near my door,

As fresh and green : 'T is even so
As through the busy world we go,
With eager eyes to see and know—
How oft we miss what lieth low !

A DARK DAY.

(NETHERWOOD.)

THERE are no daisies in the grass
    Through which I walk to-day,
Nor do I hear the little burn
    That sings beside the way.

There is no fragrance in the breeze,
    That comes from woodlands old,
No glory in the kingcups fine
    That flush the field with gold;

The violet and ladysmock
    To-day I do not see,
Nor yet the white flower of the thorn
    Nor yet the willow-tree.

A DARK DAY.

I heard the lark sing yesterday
    That all the world was fair,
Now there's a shadow on the earth
    And darkness in the air.

There are no whispers in the wood,
    No glamour in the skies,
No splendour on the forest falls,
    Nor on the river lies.

Round me I look on moorlands dim,
    A solitude so vast,
Ridge behind ridge, hill beyond hill,
    And there—behold at last

A lonely summit far away,
    One hill, the last of seven,
As it might be a cloud, a mist,
    Touched with a gleam of heaven.

All else is dark but where I see
    The far-off glory shine —
And if the darkness is my own,
    So is the splendour mine!

PRIMROSES.

"What is good for a bootless bene?"
—*Wordsworth.*

If thou art weary of sorrow,
   If thou art weary of strife,
Of all the noises of folly,
   And all the madness of life ;—
Arise in the early dawning,
   Hasten thy feet and go
Down to the briery dingle
   Where the primrose-blossoms blow.

If thou art weary of watching
   Faces so haggard and grey,
Sordid, and callous, and cunning,
   Passing thee day by day ;
Faces furrowed, and careworn,
   And loveless as thine own ;
Eyes that look out upon thee
   From the depths of a trouble unknown :

If thou art weary of pity
    For the ways of human-kind,
For the pride of the rich that are poorer
    Than beggars kinless and blind,
For the pride of knowing that knows not,
    For the boastful science of fools,
For the rattle and prattle of emptiness,
    And the wisdom of the schools;

If thou art weary of folly,
    Weary of wisdom's strife,
Weary of knowledge that cannot know
    The mystery of life;—
Arise in the early dawning,
    Hasten thy steps away,
And learn in the briery dingle
    What the primrose-blossoms say.

If thou art weary of reading
    All that is said and done,
The doleful tale of sorrow and death
    Since the making of the sun:
How the people perish in myriads,
    By famine, and fire, and flood,
Fighting the battles of guile and greed,
    In toil, and tears, and blood;

PRIMROSES.

If thou art weary of praying
    For the light of a milder day,
That peace may yet be on the earth
    Ere the heavens have passed away,
That greed may not always triumph,
    Nor cunning for ever rule,
Nor the gilded hoop of honour ring
    The forehead of a fool;

If thou art weary of sorrow,
    Weary of earth-born care,
Weary of pride and folly,
    Weary of bootless prayer;—
Arise in the early dawning,
    Hasten thy feet and go,
And learn in the briery dingle
    What the primrose-blossoms know!

MEETING STREAMS.

I KNOW a place of meeting streams,
    Where the pure waters flow,
And in a sylvan valley make
    Sweet music as they go.

These waters flow where wild-flowers grow
    The tufted ferns between,
And underneath the forest boughs,
    With all their waving green.

And oft when to that lonely place
    I fly from evil dreams,
I linger, listening to the sound,
    One sound of many streams.

And, lingering, I seem to hear,
    Far inward and divine,
A voice, as if the soul of things
    Were singing unto mine.

I know a place of meeting streams
  Where the dark waters flow
Through a close-peopled town, and make
  Strange music as they go.

By sordid homes and alleys dim,
  By haunts of crime and wrong,
These waters flow, and as they go
  They sing the same sweet song.

They whisper of the solitude
  In moorland valleys found,
They sing a song of violets
  Hid in the mossy ground.

They sing all day the old sweet song
  To woodland wanderers dear,
But in the busy hum of men
  No soul hath ears to hear.

Only when night is on the streams
  And silence in the street,
Lingering, I listen for that song
  Where the dark waters meet:

And, listening, I seem again
  To hear the mystic tone,—
As if a kindred spirit sang,
  And sang to me alone.

UNDER THE SNOW.

THE flowers, blue, golden and red,
    And the leaves of each beautiful tree
Are dead —and the summer is dead ;
And all that the poet can see
Is withered and shrivel'd and grey,
And sere with the sereness of death,
Its beauty is turned to decay,
Its odour exhaled like a breath.
The beautiful summer is dead ;
And the poet who listeneth hears
The wail of the wind overhead,
Like a voice that is sobbing in tears ;
He hears the low sound of the rain
As it weeps for each beautiful thing,
For the flowers that it fostered in vain,
And fed with the sweetness of spring ;

But when darkness is over the sky
And the poet is resting in sleep,
When the wind has forgotten to sigh,
And the rain has forgotten to weep,
From the moon-silver'd mist and the cloud,
The spirits that work in the night
Have woven a beautiful shroud
To cover the dead from his sight ;
And when he walks forth on the morrow,
In paths where he useth to go,
At once he forgetteth his sorrow
In that beautiful vision of snow !

The flowers, blue, golden and red,
And the leaves of each beautiful tree,
But not of the summer that's dead,
The eye of the poet can see,
As under the snow they lie deep,
And wait for the winds of the spring
To awaken them out of their sleep,
When the lark is beginning to sing.

The celandine, first to unfold
Its prodigal leaves to the day,
And laugh with its petals of gold,
Ere the snows have half melted away ;

The wind-flower that droops in the shade,
Like a vestal white-hooded and pure,
That hardly to heaven upraiseth her head
Or lifteth her eyelids demure ;
The purple, pale flower, that comes
With the cuckoo's earliest call :
The bell where the wild bee hums ;
And the wild rose—fairest of all
That blooms in the garden of God ;
The orchis that springeth afar ;
The daisy that loveth the sod ;
The flower that is named of a star ;
And whatever is lovely or rare
That haunteth the wood or the rill,
That maketh the fields of our childhood fair,
Or abides in the cleft of the hill ;
Not dead, but asleep—they are dreaming
In the darkness of earth, and they know
That the brightness of heaven is beaming
O'er that beautiful vision of snow !

The flowers, blue, golden and red,
And the leaves of each beautiful tree
Are dead—and they also are dead,
The friends we shall never more see ;
As the flowers, in their beauty they died,
Whose odour exhales like a breath,

And all that is left of their strength and their pride
Is sere with the sereness of death.
The children of beauty are dead ;
And the poet who listeneth hears
The wail of the wind overhead,
Like a voice that is sobbing in tears ;
He hears the low sound of the rain,
As it weeps for each beautiful one,
For the love that was fostered in vain,
For the sweetness of life that is gone.

And when darkness is over the sky,
And the poet is resting in sleep,
When the wind has forgotten to sigh,
And the rain has forgotten to weep,
Though out of the mist and the cloud,
The spirits that work in the night
Have woven a beautiful shroud
To cover the dead from his sight—
Yet he knows that the sleep that they sleep
Is not like the sleep of the flowers,
Whose dreams into beauty will leap
With the sunshine of spring, and its showers ;
And when he walks forth on the morrow,
In paths where he useth to go,
There lieth a shadow of sorrow
On that beautiful vision of snow !

FORGETFULNESS.

IT was an old man and a child
    Who gathered flowers in woodlands wild ;
Eager-looking and intent,
Through the wilderness they went,
Together now, and now asunder,
Lost to everything but wonder
Of the marvels which they found
Scattered o'er the enchanted ground,
Clothing every green recess
With primeval loveliness.

Where, beneath the sheltering trees,
Bloom the white anemones,
Where the primrose-clusters grow,
And the sweet wood-violets blow,
There I overtook the child,
And his eyes were soft and wild,
And his tiny hands were full
Of these blossoms beautiful,

FORGETFULNESS.

While his hasty feet pursued
Through the mazes of the wood
Every little wandering gleam
Beckoning through that sylvan dream.

" Little wanderer, tell me now,
Among these flowers what seekest thou?"

Looking up with wondering glee,
Strangely thus he answered me:
" My Father, who is ever kind,
Hath brought me here that I might find
A fairy child, who doth abide
Among the flowers in forests wide;
His name is Hope; and everywhere
I seek him through these vistas fair."

A little further on I found
That old man stooping to the ground
And gathering hyacinths, which he,
With tassels of the alder tree,
Did make into a posy gay,
And here and there a budding spray
Of tender green and sedges wild,
And, as he gave it to the child,
He looked from him to me and smiled
Sadly, and yet his eyes were kind:
" I knew," he said, " that we should find

FORGETFULNESS.

Whatever in this wood we sought,
And so my little boy I brought
That he might gather flowers with me,
And wandering on from tree to tree
He has found Hope as thou may'st see:
For me, too, not in vain the hours
Have passed among these leaves and flowers."

" For thee? Hast thou found Hope?" said I,
" Nay, nay, not so," he made reply ;
" Yet am I thankful none the less—
I only sought Forgetfulness !"

SUNRISE.

NEVER have the poets told us
    All the glory of the morning.
As a soul might stand in heaven
Drinking of the living fountains,
I have stood again before it,
Seen the glory of the vision,
Left behind the clouds and darkness,
And low-creeping mists of sorrow.
Many years have I been living
In the valley down below there,
Wandering in dark ways and fighting
With the shadows and the phantoms,
With the dreams and evil demons
That know not the blessed morning;
Many years until my footsteps
Had forgot the holy mountains
Where the blessed morning cometh,
Like a vision out of heaven,

SUNRISE.

When the silver gates are loosened
And the golden splendour streameth
From the tranquil summits, looking
Out on life's eternal morning.

So I came and saw the sunrise,
Saw the faint, far-coming splendour,
And I said, when life is over,
And the darkness and the shadows
Fall away, as from these summits
Fall the heavy mists and vapours
Of the night, shall we awaken
From our dreams of sin and sorrow
To a light above the darkness
Filling all the heavens with splendour;
Shall we see each other's faces,
Full of peace and full of wonder,
Wonder that we had not known it,
That the prophets had not told us
Half the marvel of the story,
How the heavens are close above us,
How the shadows are but shadows,
Of the old eternal morning.

SUMMER DAYS.

A LITTLE nook of wilderness,
  Between the meadow and the river,
Where two erewhile together came,
And one will come no more forever.

The rustic bridge, the narrow road,
The seat upon the fallen pine,
The whisper of the summer woods,
So sweet, but not so sweet as thine.

A little wild-flower long ago
Among the tangled grasses grew,—
So many things are dead since then,
How should not that be withered too?

Here where we sat I sit alone,
Watching until the sun goes down,
For though 't is summer time to-day,
To-morrow will the woods be brown.

'Year after year,' the poet sang,
Year after year the spirit sighs,
And summer days will come again,
And suns will set in summer skies,—

But to this bourne of wilderness
Between the meadow and the river,
Will any come because we came,
And say,—They come no more forever!

CHANGE.

THE tree is the same,
    But I am not he who came
At mornings, at noons and at eves,
Looking up with delight at the beautiful leaves,
At the summer green and the autumn gold,
In the times of old.

HAUNTED.

ALL night, as one who dreameth,
    I lay in a room alone,
And ever the chimes were chiming,
And ever a wind would moan.

I lay in a haunted chamber,
And I saw in the darkness there
A face that was fairer than life or love
And sadder than my despair.

And I said, as one who crieth
To God with prayerful breath,
"Hast thou no angel of pity,
But only the angel of death?"

I lay as one who dreameth,
And out of the silence came
A voice whose music throbbed like fire
Through all my listening frame.

"Yea, death is an angel of pity,
He will bring thy heart to mine,
And till that angel calleth thee
My soul shall wait for thine."

And in the cold, white morning
I knelt and asked a boon,
"Madonna, pray that He may send
The angel of pity soon!"

SHADOWS.

OUT of the old house into the new—
    Heed not the shadows that beckon and
        mourn ;
Leave them alone to the sorrows they knew ;
    Never to them or the sorrows return.

Ah, but the shadows are everywhere,
    Still to thy footsteps their footsteps are true ;
What if the shadows should follow thee there
    Out of the old house into the new !

NIGHT COMETH.

THE day is dying,
   The voices cease,
The night brings silence,
   And silence peace.

The coming and going
   Is at an end,
The meeting and parting,
   ' My friend,'—' My friend !'

The faithful fingers
   Begin to tire,
A wan face watches
   A dying fire.

The sleepless vigils,
   The lonely tears,
Are buried away
   In the silent years.

NIGHT COMETH.

The toil is ended,
  The duty done,
The passion wasted,
  The patience won.

The ways are lonely,
  The farewell said,
The night is silent,
  The day is dead.

AN UNKNOWN BOURNE.

KIND voice, and so sweet,
   Dear moments, so fleet,
Sad parting, to meet
     At an unknown bourne.

Light dies o'er the fell,
Low winds through the dell
Are sighing farewell
     From an unknown bourne.

Sad voice, that must pray,
Till dawn rises grey,
And winds die away
     To an unknown bourne.

Sweet patience is best,
Sweet slumber is blest,
So wayfarers rest
     At an unknown bourne.

NIGHTSHADE.

"And out of the good of evil born
   Came Uriel's voice of cherub scorn."
                                    Emerson.

AS I went by a wayside lonely
   I found a trodden flower,
An outcast of the wilderness,
And I took it for my dower.

It was not fair to look upon,
As the world of fairness deems,
But to him who knows its secret
It gives the power of dreams.

It lives not in the summer,
When the sky is blue and bright,
But when the year is dying,
And it blooms in the shade of night.

It is poor, and prone and barren,
A weed of waste and shame,
It shrinks away from the sunshine,
But it fills the dark with flame.

It haunts not in the meadow
Among the cups of gold,
But creeps below the hagthorntree,
Where the homeless wind blows cold.

Not in the lordly woodlands,
Nor in the gardens fair,
Among the glad red roses,
They do not find it there.

Nor with the pale, proud lilies
Has it been known to dwell,
But where the lost, sad outcasts go
Down through the gates of hell.

Not knowing why, I took it
From the dust beneath my shoon,
And, knowing now, I prize it
Beyond the sun and moon;

For, though foul, and weird and loathsome,
To all the world it seems,
To him who knows its mystery
It gives the power of dreams.

WHITHER?

OUR hearts abide in patience,
    Knowing the end will come;
Our tired footsteps wander,
    Until they find a home.

Our eyes grow dim with watching
    And weary of their quest;
Weary, but uncomplaining,
    We journey to our rest.

Through life and death we journey,
    Through all the barren years,
Beneath the silent heavens
    That smile upon our tears;

We come forth out of darkness
    And into darkness go,—
But whence, O soul, and whither,
    Not even the angels know!

A STILL SMALL VOICE.

O SOUL, I said to my soul one day,
　　Thou goest with me a toilsome way ;
Art thou not weary of all that is done,
Of all that is suffer'd, beneath the sun ?
Art thou not tired of the strife and hate,
And the terrible ways of the unknown fate,
Of labour and endless misery
For the myriads who breed, and feed and die,
And know no glory in earth or sky ?
Art thou not tired of thine own poor share
Of the tangle of thought, of the burden of care,
Of the blind world's hope and its blind despair ;
Of truth that is ever one half a lie ;
Of the poor, proud virtue that sitteth so high
And says to its God, ' I am Thine, and they
Who grovel beneath in the mire and clay
Belong to the Devil that ruleth below ?'—
Art thou not weary of all that we know,
Of science that bringeth the world to light,
An empty bubble blown in the night,

By Whom it hath never a name to name!
Of all that we do for love or fame,
By passion driven, at duty's call,
Art thou not weary, my soul, of all?

And my soul made answer,—Nay, not so!
There is something more which thou dost not know.
Thou speakest as one in a troubled dream
Of things that are not what they seem.
With thee in the world there is sorrow and sin,
And passion and pain, but here within,
In the life I live with God apart,
There is peace beyond the prayer of thy heart.
I know how dark are the ways of thy feet,
Where terror, and strife and agony meet,
Where thou wanderest far on a hopeless quest,
Now praying for light, now longing for rest,
Now stumbling on, thou knowest not where,
Bearing thy burden of thought and care.
But think not that evil is evil alone,
That sorrow is only that sorrow may groan.
If all were all that thine eyes can see,
If thought had never a mystery,
What comfort could'st thou ask of me—
What hope that all will yet be well?—
Thou knowest I know what I may not tell.

BY WAYS UNKNOWN.

A WANDERING outcast seeks his home,
   From far-off climes his footsteps roam,
He seeks it over land and sea,
Yet knows not where that home may be;
He meets his kindred far and near,
Who seek like him that home so dear;
He hears their voices in the street,
So sweet—so more than music sweet!
He knows them by their faithful eyes,
That greet his own with glad surprise;
Wistful he lingers by the way,
And fain by theirs his feet would stay,
But each must wander forth alone,
And find his home by ways unknown.
He cannot tell how this should be,
But such he knows is heaven's decree.
He murmurs not at destiny;
And when one whispers, 'stay awhile!'
He answers, with a loving smile,

' Not here, not here, may we who meet
A moment now with weary feet,
With feet however weary, rest;
Go thou upon thy lonely quest,
Far parted as from east to west,
Although our wandering feet must turn,
We journey to the self-same bourne,
As these horisons, wide and vast,
Meet in one shining heaven at last,
So thy true heart and mine, my friend,
Shall meet where life's dim pathways end.'

And when the wanderer is come
Alone and weary to his home,
'T is said he knows it not, but lies
Down on the threshold, and his eyes
Are dark with slumber, and in sweet
And tranquil rest his pilgrim-feet
Are folded, and his soul has peace :
And so his lonely wanderings cease ;
And dreaming by the silent door
That all the weary quest is o'er,
Behold, the spirits of his kin
Come forth,— and bear the dreamer in !

EDEN.

AMONG the distant mountains,
    Beneath the setting sun,
There is a lonely Eden
    Where peace may yet be won.

And deep within the forest
    There bloom enchanted bowers,
Beyond the gleaming vistas,
    Where joy may yet be ours.

And by the winding river,
    Far-shining in the west,
There is a Land of Beulah,
    Where wandering souls may rest.

O, if we could but find it,
    By forest or by stream,
That land, that lonely Eden,
    And find it not a dream!

A LONELY RIVER.

I WAIT by a lonely river,
    I walk in a lonely land,
Where skies are fair forever
    And all the hills are grand.

Where skies are fair forever,
    I stand in the lonely ways,
I come and go by a river,
    In glamour of nights and days.

I wait by a lonely river,
    I hear the waters roll,
And sweet will be forever
    The music in my soul.

Where skies are fair forever
    And all the hills are grand,
I come and go by a river,
    That sings in a lonely land.

VIATICUM.

YOU go to morning service,
    I wander by the way ;
You love to hear the preacher,
    I what the wild-birds say.

You in the solemn singing
    A sweet assurance find,
I hear an ancient prophecy
    Whose voice is in the wind.

To you the Book is holy,
    The promise of His word,
Sacred to me the solitude
    Wherein I meet my Lord.

You in the chancel kneeling,
    To God in Christ draw near,
I go alone—to Him alone—
    And find the Comforter.

INWARD LIGHT.

SOLE star that in the sunset burns,
    The hour, but not the dream, returns,
  My dream of years gone by,
When the white glory of thy ray
Seemed of a purer, lovelier day
    Than this of earth and sky.

Thou art not now a presence fair,
A living splendour of the air,
    A sentinel of heaven,
To whom a nearer glimpse of Him
Who hides beyond the ether dim
    Than to our life is given.

I cry not with a lonely cry
That thou art nearer the Most High,
    Who buildeth there alone,
Beyond the utmost void, and far
Beyond the glimmer of a star,
    His solitary throne.

And yet I walk not in the night
Unvisited of purest light,
   To cheer my lonely way ;
But not from rolling orb, or sphere,
From radiant cloud, or azure clear,
   Descends the mystic ray.

And what this hallowed light may be,
From what far bourne it comes to me,
   To me is all unknown :
A sudden gleam, a glory sweet,
Is often with me in the street
   And when I walk alone.

I may not know, I cannot tell
How in my soul it comes to dwell,
   Or how it comforts me :
'T is not in thought or vision rare,
'T is not in language to declare
   Its pure felicity.

Some say it is a living beam
Of inmost heaven, and some a dream
   That leads we know not where,
But where it leads me I must go,
No light in all this night of woe
   Like this to me is fair.

INWARD LIGHT.

Star of the soul! my way is dark,
But if at times thy kindling spark
   With mystic radiance shine,
My pain is peace, my sorrow prayer,
And deeper than my deep despair
   A sympathy divine.

THE KING'S GARDEN.

THERE are flowers of light in the King's
    Garden,
  White flowers of a land unseen,
There are flowers of peace in the King's Garden,
  And paths of peace between.

I know not where is the King's Garden,
  But this I surely know,
Soft fragrance of its heavenly blooms
  Haunts me where'er I go.

There is no way to the King's Garden
  Far down in the dawning white,
No way in the paths of the setting sun,
  Nor under the stars of night;

But over the wild and over the wold,
  When the winds of God blow free,
From tranquil bowers in the King's Garden
  Sweet balms are borne to me.

There is no gate to the King's Garden,
    No lofty bourne or bound,
No beaten path or perilous
    O'er that enchanted ground ;

But I walk in the light of the King's Garden,
    And all the ways are sweet
With fragrance of its heavenly flowers
    Around my weary feet.

ASPHODELS.

"That's for thoughts."
— *Shakespeare.*

I BROUGHT my flowers to the market,
   For market-folk to prize,
Dear as the love of faithful hearts,
   The light of faithful eyes :

I brought the flowers I had gathered
   In many a haunted dell,
Under the purple mornings,
   Into the street to sell :

Some in midsummer dreams had seen
   The forest fairies dance,
And some a charmèd life had known
   In gardens of romance ;

Some in blind ways of fear and strife
    Of painful thought were born,
Some found a home in desert caves,
    Where sorrow lives forlorn;

And some had comforted the feet
    That rest beneath the sod;
And some had kissed the pilgrim shoon,
    Sweet with the dews of God;

Some knew the song of the evening star,
    The song of the stars of prime,
The song of winds that sing of the sea,
    Of the sea that sings of time;

And some had heard a sylvan pipe,
    In years when love was a child,
And some the harps of wandering bards
    Upon a homeless wild.

I had gathered some in the sunshine
    Of lost and lovelier years,
And some in a time of solitude,
    And some in a place of tears.

From many a holy mountain,
  From many a fairy grove,
I brought them to the market-folk
  To sell my flowers for love :

Far-wandering weeds of Eden,
  Pure blooms of Arcady,
All for a little price of love,
  If any love might be.

But they were poor of aught but gold,
  No other price had they,
And for a sordid boon they took
  And threw my flowers away.

Lilies of light and loveliness
  They cast into the street,
Garlands of Eros and the Muse
  Were dust beneath their feet.

So sadly from the market-place,
  Where Mammon buys and sells,
I go along my lonely way,
  And gather Asphodels.

RHYMES AND DAYS.

"What see'st thou else, in the dark backward
and abysm of time?"
—*Shakespeare.*

CHILDHOOD.

'TIS well that Childhood has its own delight,
    That unto common things it can impart
The freshness and the joy of its own heart;
As the young dawn to the grey mists of night

Lends beauty not their own. Even with such light
Upon them do my earliest memories start
From the dark past; familiar things, a part
Of common life, yet do they seem as bright

As gleams from some pre-natal paradise;
Such are my first maternal memories,
The daisied grass, the woodland walks that seem,

Though now well known, like places in a dream,
Far in a world of faerie mystery,—
For such was this untrodden world to me.

BOYHOOD.

HE is a very Quixote, and will fleet
    The time in dreams, and dreaming he will see
Come riding forth the knights of chivalry,
With golden helm, and plume of victory!

And in another mood, he oft will sit
Whole summer days beneath the forest trees,
Weaving romances, talking poesies:
'T is his prerogative all that Fancy sees

To realise, and still, as comes the fit,
Be Alexander o'er the world prevailing,
Bright-armed Achilles the great Hector
    quailing,

Ulysses through the dim sea ever sailing,
The lonely Crusoe in his island-hold,
Or the poor Pilgrim to the City of Gold.

FRIENDSHIP.

'TIS nature's finest, rarest harmony,
    When souls congenial think and speak of things
For which the wise world cares not, and each brings
His mind's chief treasures for the mutual eye

Of kindred thought to brood on lovingly :
Book-memories dear and sweet imaginings
That soar on speculation's fearless wings
Through all the universe of mystery

And marvel wide, of human hope and fear.
Eugene ! such pleasures pure with thee alone
My spirit 'mid life's alien throng hath known ;

And do we live and not regret that year
Should follow year, and thought's rich harvests lie
Ungathered, or the spoil of each dull passer by.

ASPIRATION.

WHOSE thoughts in sympathy with nature move
In all her forms, whoever, wonder-eyed,
Finds constant pleasure in her marvels wide,
Still seeking to exalt himself above

Low cares, and blind pursuits, and selfish love,
And sensual sloth, although by fate denied
To gain in seats of academic pride
Thy classic lore, O Muse, if thou approve

And teach him all the mysteries divine
Of sense and soul, albeit all unknown
To the world's praise or blame, he may to thine

Inspiring harmonies attune his own
Self-pleasing thoughts and intuitions fine,
" Making sweet solace to himself alone."

EVENSONG.

'TIS better, sweet, to lose, yet still adore thee,
　　Than to have found thee not the soul I
　　　sought.
Thine image, as I last beheld thee, wrought
By memory's wizard power, is before me.

'T was evening in the church, through windows
　　dim
Streamed the rich gold of sunset, the loud hymn
Up-pealing like the song of Seraphim.
And on thy lovely face that sunset shone,

And o'er thy vestments, and upon thy hair,
And thou who wert before so passing fair
Seemed now an angel, singing in the sun.

That vision pure will never pass away,
Time that will change thee, never can decay
The summer brightness of that Sabbath day.

AFTER MANY YEARS.

AND we have met thus after many years ;
    Have met as strangers, and have parted so,
Without a word of all our hopes and fears
Since parting last, a weary while ago.

I know 't is vain to mourn that parting now,
'T was well for thee—and me—for we had need
Of that cold fortitude that does endow
Cold hearts with care of all that worldlings heed.

That dream of ours, that time, is dead and gone,
The hopes are dead on which we then did live,
And I am now content to be alone ;

Yet for our poor dream's sake, I could but grieve
That we, who once each others' hearts did know,
Should meet as strangers—parting even so.

A PORTRAIT.

SO like, so sweet, so beautiful is this
    Fair semblance in its pure serenity,
That I do seem her very self to see ;
And yet fond, faithful memory doth miss

Many a transient gleam of loveliness,—
The light that speaks and kindles in the eye,
The earnest glance of quiet sympathy,
The bright, frank smile, that would sometimes
    express

More than the subtilest language can disclose
Of feeling's intricate life, and yet how fair,
In its expression of the still repose

Of a most womanly soul, this portrait shows :
So like, so beautiful, and gazing there
Who would not dream of love—and who for care
    would care !

THE LOST PILGRIM.

THERE was a Pilgrim once, whose journey lay
    Through climes of various aspect, some were fair
And full of all delight, some wild and bare,
Fear-peopled, mountain regions, by the way

Where furies haunt and vultures seek their prey ;
Behoved him then in all things to prepare
That he might wisely do, not rashly dare.
But the poor fool was tempted to delay

In those soft climes, wasting his heart away
In blind pursuit of pleasure, boasting vain
He would at his own time make bold essay

Upon those deserts and their bourne attain :
Ah, surely folly never will grow old—
His bones are bleaching on the mountains cold!

THE DEAD YEARS.

LOOK not behind thee, turn thou not thine eye
To the dead past, for there thou wilt behold
All the dead years, like corpses, stark and cold,
Lie withering in the moonless winds that sigh

Through the dark realm of mortal destiny.
They came to me, and on their plumes of gold
Bore golden boon; they greeted me with bold,
And boundless, and most glorious prophecy;

They gave me gifts that did to me appear
Divine—love, genius, all-sympathy—
The key of Heaven and Hades. Woe is me!

The gold plumes faded, as each dying year
Passed, and, with mocking wail and maniac stare,
Turned its dead face unto the starless air!

FOREBODINGS.

IF from the steep ascent of thirty years
    I could look forward to the time to come,
Would the dim shape of the on-speeding doom
Fulfil my hopes, or justify my fears?

Vain question: if in the future aught appears
Uncertain, leave it to its friendly gloom,
Nor seek to frame in fancy thine own tomb.
There is a certainty that still upbears

The soul like a great ship amid the sea,
Whose calm course mocks the waves'
        inconstancy.
It is the law on which all being rides;

It is the power that in all change abides;
It is the Soul of things—the Soul of me—
It is the one, the only certainty.

ACCUSATION.

WHY dost thou blame me that I have not been
Friends with the world, living as other men,
Accepting all its discipline of pain,
Sharing in its rough toils, nor deeming mean

Its homely pleasures? But the way serene
Is not through these, which all may not attain.
For some there be the high gods do ordain
To wander lonely in the world, wherein

They have been cast too early, or too late;
Nature that frames the oak to bear the weight
Of stormy centuries, and sometimes showers

On the dead year unseasonable flowers,
To wither there; thus orders man's estate :
Therefore accuse not me—nor will I Fate.

HUMILITY.

I DO not judge the world: how should I so?
    That many good and lovely things there be
Even in its dreariest wastes of misery,
And in its dens of selfish pride, I know.

And yet I would that fate had bid me go
Some quiet path from all its tumult free,
In the sweet valley of Humility,
Not far from where immortal flowers blow,

In many a muse- and fairy-peopled dell
At foot of Parnass, from whose steeps sublime
I might hear strains of song that ever swell

Around each genius-haunted pinnacle;
Or in sweet commune fleet the hallowed time
With visitants from its serenest clime.

AN OLD BOOK.

OLD Book, of many legends thou hast told,
    Yet thine own secret keepest passing well;
Sly, monkish teacher in thy cloistered cell,
That only what is written dost unfold,

And thine own hidden knowledge keep'st like
    gold,
That Mammon guards with many a niggard spell.
Ah, if I could but win thee now to tell
Of the sage beards communed with thee of old,

And all that passed between you of dark lore,
Forbidden; or of beauty's bower retired,
Where white hands clasped thee, where bright
    eyes admired

And made thee proud with tears, lips whispered
    o'er
Thy words in music, lips that might have fired
The souls of all the anchorites of yore.

MY GARDEN.

FAREWELL! I have delayed me here too long
   In this poor garden of my idleness,
Seeking to rear its lowly flowers in peace,
When all around me clamoured the fierce throng

Of toiling multitudes; and now among
Its pleasant paths with careless feet they press,
As though they deemed it but a wilderness
Of weeds; and now they hurry me along,

Trampling my fences frail. 'T was the world's
      wrong,
And mine, from the great doom to shrink afraid,
That bindeth man to man for mutual aid,

Trifling with selfish aims; while with a strong
And steadfast heart I should have joined the strife
Through which man struggles to a nobler life.

WASTE PLACES.

WHY do the silver archways of the morn,
    Why do the radiant sunsets rise up-piled
In splendour above splendour, o'er the wild,
Untrodden wastes, the solitudes forlorn ;

Or build their golden roofs, as if in scorn,
O'er clownish heads ; why sleep the moonbeams
    mild
In alpine vales ; where eyes have never smiled
Upon their beauty, why are wildflowers born ;

While many an eye is pining to behold
The glory that is ever-more unseen
In lonely places, desolate and cold ?

Why has it thus with beauty ever been,
That it shall never, never, be the dower
Of those who love it most, most feel its heavenly
    power ?

A STAR.

A STAR shines on me from the darkening
    years,
Amid the wintry solitude appears
A presence clothed in beauty's brightest dress,
And with its pure and perfect loveliness

Awakes my spirit from its dream of pain,
That on the wearied wings of hope would fain
Soar from night of its despair afar
Towards the sphere of that self-radiant star.

And should it vanish from the tranquil air,
Ere I ascend above the storm, to where,
Serenely gliding on its path of light,

Its presence maketh beautiful the night;
Yet still I shall not all in vain have striven,
If its ray guide me to a calmer heaven.

BROTHER AND SISTER.

IT was thy life-long prayer, this side the tomb
   That you should meet once more: 'T was
       not to be;
That sister dear, who in thy memory
Was still a maiden in her village home,

Far off, unseen, lived all her years to come
And died, by children mourned unknown to thee.
O Love, O Death, the end of all we see,
But not of all we cannot see, the dumb,

Dim world of dream and prophecy !
Must love like this be unfulfilled for ever ?
Or are there holier fields, a happier sky,

Upon the far shore of that dark, cold river,
Where these true hearts have met at last and
       found
That endless love with endless life is crowned ?

HEAVENLY LOVE.

IF it be human for the Human Heart
    To express the passion of its grief in prayer
And we may hope that they, who once did care
For our well-being here, may still have part

In the eternal Providence ; if they,
By heaven permitted, still may seek to be
Helpers of those for whom undyingly
Their love still burns ; then gladly would I pray

To thee, O sorrow-sainted Mother, mine,
Doing and suffering much, who still did hold
Thy soul obedient to the law divine,

In all life's troubles, dark and manifold :
If Heaven is Love, as saints and sages say,
Thine is of Heaven, and will not pass away.

COMPENSATION.

LAST of thy father's children, thou hast passed
    The threshold of the years of womanhood:
A mingled yarn—good, evil, evil, good—
Thou find'st this life in which our lot is cast.

Even youth is not all flowers and summer shining,
And there are flowers that whither ere their prime;
Bid brief farewell then to the morning time,
And go upon thy way without repining.

For in the coming years is compensation
For whatsoe'er shall with the past decay,
Those influences of a maturer day

That gladden and exalt the humblest station;
Ripening the impulsive feelings of the mind
To thoughtful sympathy with all mankind.

BEREAVEMENT.

DEAR Child! of much the mournful past did hold
Of most sweet promising, thou sole remain;
Last severed link of a time-broken chain,
That erst did bind affections manifold

Of loving hearts, now silent in the mould,
Too soon by death's fast following arrows slain;
Thy coming was a joy, thy going pain;
For being here, in thee I did behold

A vision of the past, thy every tone,
Though wording present meanings, told alone
Of those departed ones whom we shall see

About us never more; thou wert a light,
In whose soft radiance things o'er which the night
Had gathered were revealed again to me.

REGRETS.

AND now thy voice is silent as a dream—
'T was but a moment, and 't is heard no more—
And silence shrouds the grave as heretofore.
Thy brief, bright coming was a transient gleam

That did the past from the past time redeem.
'T is gone, I am alone, and, as before,
Remaineth nought of all that precious store
Of things departed, but an outworn theme,

Which brooding memory unto sorrow sings,
Of old, familiar, half-forgotten things,
Of passionate regrets and pitying tears,

Impatient thoughts of that old, happy time,
And prayer—that thou mayest in thy coming prime
Find recompense for thy bereaved years.

WAITING.

THE night was dark with clouds, the heavy rain
Flooded the silent street, against the pane
Drifted the storm, a wide wind rose around
The roof and eaves, with wonder-waking sound;

And now it was a low hymn for the dying,
A wailing for the dead, a sad voice crying
To the mute heavens, and now an answering tone,
As of one singing to the stars alone

A song of sweet and solemn mystery.
So came the wind and went alternately,
For now again round the dark eaves 't would moan,

Whispering its secret to the earless stone;
And in the pause of the storm they came and said,
As we sat silent, listening, "She is dead!"

VISION.

SINCE then a vision in my mind has been
    A form all white and silent I have seen
Of one lying alone who erst beguiled
Many an hour in talk with us and smiled

As the good only smile who ever wear
White hope when others wrap them in despair.
And out in the dark night, around the room
Where she is lying cold, that wind will come,

Wailing; and now, methinks, it seemeth why;
And so when it upriseth to the sky,
Like the far rushing of angelic wings,

I listen for the mystery it sings;
And though nor joy, nor sorrow, as before—
Yet answereth it my hope— and answereth more.

REALITY.

MY fears were more than the reality,—
    The silence-sealèd lip, the sunken eye,
The pallid, frozen cheek, the forehead cold,
These were what I had dreaded to behold:

But when the shroud was lifted in mute awe,
I saw not these, and yet the dead I saw:
But the still aspect where no trace of care
Now lingers, all so passionless and fair,

And the deep silence, and the dreamless ease,
The quiet of an unimagined peace,
The perfect calm, without or pulse or breath,

Revealed the presence of benignest death,—
The great, white angel of the tranquil mien,
That brooded there, with shadowy wing serene

EVANGELIST.

I.

THE holiest aspect of angelic light,
  That veils its spiritual loveliness
Before the mystery of God, could less
Move my deep heart with reverence than the sight

Of this beloved face with all delight.
Without a guide, through doubt's dark wilderness
I stumbled in blind fear, with meaningless
And babbling tongues that call amid the night

Confused, with phantoms of unreal woe
Haunted, until his voice rose clear and low,
And musical with thoughts that come and go

Between man's heart and heaven, and led me where,
Above the mists of error and despair,
The light of heavenly hope makes all things fair.

II.

And so with sweet, sad tears mine eyes are dim,
For gazing on this countenance divine,
By all rare powers and feelings moulded fine,
I think 't is all I e'er shall see of him

Who from dark teachings did my heart redeem,
Who from his high removed sphere to mine
Shed influences that hallow and refine ;
Soothing my sadness with some cheerful theme,

Or with some high, immortal tale, inwrought
With rarest fancy and with purest thought;
And more—oh, infinitely more—whose bold,

Yet consecrated hand, did all remove
From sweet religion's name the jargons old ;
For all his creed was this—that God is love.

YORICK.

"One writ with me in sour misfortune's book."
— *Shakespeare.*

I.

ALAS, poor Yorick! oft would'st thou repeat
These mournful words in a self-soothing tone,
"Peace waits us on the shores of Acheron!"
Dark days were thine, companionships unmeet;

Falsehood and fear perplexed thy wandering feet;
The far-off ways of light to thee were known,
But thou had'st not the strength to walk alone,
Nor friend to help with counsel wise and sweet.

And the blind guides, whose eyes are like the night,
Who call light darkness and the darkness light,
What help hadst thou to hope from such as they?

What hope to cheer thee on thy lonely way?
Save this, the last sad refuge of despair,
At the blind end of things, that peace is there!

II.

So thou did'st say, "peace waits us" in the grave ;
When no kind voice was near to soothe and
　　bless,
This was thy only hope—thy hopelessness !—
The one poor boon which thou of heaven did'st
　　crave.

And this last prayer of broken hearts, the slave
Of creeds as dark as they are pitiless,
Would dare deny to human wretchedness,
Denying God's good will and power to save.

But we—We know so little, and the wise
Are dumb before these awful mysteries—
But we may hope that sorrow such as thine

May hide from love's own tears a Love Divine ;
May be a blindness on the spirit thrown
From a too inward radiance of its own !

ORSINI.
1858.

LOW lies Orsini's head! Justice hath claimed
    Her victim and revenge is satisfied,
By the cold hand of death the heroic pride
Of that unquailing spirit has been tamed!

Ye, who have sat around your fires and blamed
The fierce and reckless deed for which he died,
Which tyrants execrate and slaves deride,
Think of his wrongs whene'er his crime is named;

Think of his wanderings, hunted by the foes
Who fill the dungeons of his native land
With all her best and bravest, of the woes

Of hopeless durance, while his fettered hand
Yearned to avenge the cause of Italy—
Content for her to live, for her to die!

AT HURSTWOOD.

DID Colin Clout walk here beside the Brun,
  Musing his shepherd rhymes? And is it true
These were the hills, the "wasteful hills," he knew—
Bleak Pendle, Boulsworth, Thievely, Hambledon?

Is this small stream the Muses' Helicon ;
These valleys low the "savage soil" where grew
That flower of poesy, which, with the few
That never fade, looks upward to the sun,

Filling the world with fragrance? Never owned
Nor Greece nor Italy a sweeter flower,
So golden-petal'd, radiant, richly zoned

In the green leafage of its fairy bower ;—
Yet Colin, piping on his oaten reed,
Poor Colin found it here a forest weed!

Photo. Geo. Hy. Foulds.] "SPENSER'S HOUSE" AT HURSTWOOD. [Painting by S. Austerberry.

A KEEPSAKE.

IF thou wouldst keep with care
A treasure rich and rare
Of all sweet things and fair,—
The memories of the dead
Our love has hallowèd;
All brightness in the past
Time has not quite o'ercast;
What visitings there be
Of living sympathy,
Of friendship and of love;
All influences that move
The world's humanity
As winds upon the sea;
Whatever nature yields
Of the fair life of fields,
The leafy rest of woods,
The mountain solitudes,

Or the serene of heaven;
Whatever more is given
Unto the poet's eye
Than life's reality,
Fairer than nature's glory,
More marvellous than story,
Of deeper truth than aught
Into pure knowledge wrought
By man's aspiring thought,
And to whose good the best
That love deems holiest
Is but a childhood's learning,—
Symbol, and dream, and yearning
By which the poet teaches
What science never reaches—
Of fairy life and lone,
Of wonder-lands unknown,
Of spirit-realms afar
Beyond the furthest star,
Where care and sorrow cease
And life is love and peace.

If these to thee are dear
Let them have record here,
That so, this book of thine
May be the priceless shrine

A KEEPSAKE.

Of all sweet memories ;
And keep, for sake of these,
What else would only be
A poor—Remember me !

FORGETMENOT.

SHE gave me of her hair
    A little shining curl
That hung behind her ear,
    White—whiter than the pearl.

Silent, with drooping lids,
    The precious gift she brought,
And with its braid was twined
    The blue forgetmenot.

That little flower is dead
    This many and many a year,
But on the silken tress
    The light is soft and clear.

'T is well love's symbol there
    I can at will restore,
But not one thread of wandering gold
    Ever— forever more!

EVENING SHADOWS.

THE evening shadows fall
  Athwart the pathways old,
Where underneath the branches broad
Of these fair trees we stroll'd,
In years that come no more.

I listen to the same
Still murmur of the stream,
Whose soft, low burden haunted us—
The music of a dream
That will return no more.

The last note of the thrush
I hear—the beetle's drone—
The rustle of my own slow steps—
But ah! the silvery tone
Of that dear voice no more.

Trembles the star of eve
From the same azure skies,
But its ethereal loveliness,
Mirror'd in lovelier eyes,
I shall behold no more.

THE TWO SPIRITS.

THERE is a spirit in thine eyes,
    A spirit of sorrow and tears,
That seems to mourn for the destinies
    That come with the coming years.

But another spirit is in thy voice,
    And it says to the spirit of tears,
'There is joy in the present and I rejoice,
    And hope in the coming years.'

May the spirit of joy abide with thee
    To the end of the coming years,
That so thy life may never be
    Alone with the spirit of tears!

A NIGHT-WATCH.

I WATCH the night alone,
With the shadows I remember,
And the rain beats dark December,
And the night-winds moan.

And the shadows come and go,
Phantom shapes upon the ceiling,
Phantom faces by me stealing,
As the fire burns low.

As the dying embers fall,
Shapes and shadows dim and fleeting
Come with old, familiar greeting,
Sad and silent all.

And sometimes it may be,
When the night is dead and lonely,
That my own dark shadow only
Keeps its watch with me.

And out there in the rain,
While around the world is dreaming,
Comes a wistful face, soft gleaming,
To the window pane.

And out there in the blue,
Over lonely hills wide ranging,
Go my faithful friends, unchanging,
True, forever true.

So fleet the phantoms grey,
They are lovely but unreal,
Youthful hopes and dreams ideal,
Passing swift away.

And so I watch alone,
With the shadows I remember,
And the rain beats dark December,
And the night-winds moan.

A SONG OF REST.

WHEN the day's work is done
  Shall not the toiling one
Go to his quiet home,
  There to find rest?
When the long night is come
  Shall he not rest?

When the cold limbs are stark,
When the shut eye is dark,
When the closed ear is dead,
  Is there not rest?
When the last prayer is said
  Is there not rest?

Harder the toil has been,
Longer the day between
Dawning and dark to thee,
  Sweeter the rest.
Calmer the night shall be,
  Deeper the rest.

A SONG OF REST.

What though the fortunate,
Mocking thy meaner fate,
Flaunt thee with idle state,
   Taking their rest,
'Tis but an hour to wait,
   Thou shalt have rest.

Fear not thy destiny,
Heed not the zealot's cry,
Leave him alone to rave,
   Go to thy rest;
Sweet will the wild grass wave
   Over thy rest.

A SONG OF HEROES.
1857.

WE need not search the scrolls of time
 Or old historic lands
For deeds of daring more sublime
 Than English hearts and hands
Have wrought in India's fiery clime,
 Oppressed by servile bands
Of foes, whose more than rebel crime
 Reeks from their myriad hands.

Nor need we go to those old days
 When chivalry arose,
And knightly valour did amaze
 Our ancient Paynim foes :
For ne'er might warlike feats outblaze,
 In brightest glory, those
On which an Indian sun doth gaze,
 From Himalayan snows.

Since Richard Cœur-de-Lion's sword
  His foes with terror struck;
Since Cromwell gave the battle-word
  O'er Dunbar's sea-bound rock:
Since Wellington's calm voice was heard
  'Mid cannon's earthquake shock;
No soldier's name our hearts has stirred
  Like thine, bold Havelock!

Hope of the brave, when dangers lower—
  Be still their guiding star!
Remember those in peril's hour,
  From friends and help afar,
Women and babes who shrieking cower
  In tears and blood—nor spare—
But strike with sword of vengeful power,
  O thunder-bolt of war!

For Havelock, bravest of the brave;
  Wilson, of Delhi won;
For Eyre, the scourge of many a slave
  Whose crimes have stained the sun;
For noble Inglis who did save
  Our Lucknow garrison;
Shout! But be silent o'er the grave
  Of Neil and Nicholson.

Chamberlain, our Murat the bold;
  Greathed, Greatheart shall be;
Lawrence and Wheeler, Romans old,
  Who died when Rome was free;
And in the lists of fame enrolled,
  The name of Willoughby
Shall rank with his who backward rolled
  Porsenna's chivalry!

But let these haughty vauntings cease!
  For far, O Skene, above
The proudest tales of Rome and Greece,
  Thy pass of death shall prove.
Song, legend, history, no piece
  Of passion has to move
The human soul like that wild kiss
  Of anguish and of love,

Which thou didst give to her who stood
  Undaunted by thy side,
When, all athirst for lust and blood,
  The banded traitors tried
Their strength in vain—the rebel brood
  Were baffled, while the tide
Of onset bravely you withstood—
  And then—as bravely—died!

Yet not alone to names so great
    I dedicate the lay;
But to the humblest soldier's fate
    Who, in that perilous fray,
Shall strike one stroke for those who wait,
    In mangled heaps, the day
When robèd priests in solemn state
    Their burial rites shall say.

'T is said the chivalry of old
    We never more shall see,
That we have made the idol gold
    Our only deity:
Yet still, I trust, beat hearts as bold
    'Neath garbs of low degree,
As e'er 'neath armour's princely fold
    Throbb'd high for victory!

They rest in peace who bravely fell!
    And honoured to all time,
Their names shall be the magic spell
    Of many a deathless rhyme.
And when the bards their stories tell,
    In epic page sublime,
By English voices shall the tale
    Be sung in every clime.

LULLABY.

> "Mine I loved, and mine I praised,
> And mine that I was proud on."
> —*Shakespeare.*

DEATH met my darling in the street,
    And lifted up his little feet
And bore him, singing lullaby,
And softly murmured, 'Come with me,
And let me kiss thee on the face
And lay thee in a quiet place,
From danger far and far from fear,
That wait around thy footsteps here.
Thou knowest not and canst not know
The weary road thy feet would go,
Too rough, and perilous and wild
For such as thee, my gentle child.

Come, let us go, I have a nest,
Quiet and safe, where thou shalt rest.
Come, let us go, and make our home
Where fear and danger cannot come
In that still house where I abide—
The way is dark, the world is wide!'

And so Death took him from my door,
And I who mourned now mourn no more;
In pity took him, as it seems,
From evil and from evil dreams,
Shadows that meet me by the way,
That walk with me from day to day,
And weary me with clamour vain
For him who will not come again :
For all so soon as death was gone,
Came Sorrow, making bitter moan,
And look'd at me with hollow eye;
And then pale Pain came wandering by,
And spectral Fears, and sordid Cares,
Mischances, Agonies, Despairs,
All shapes of misery and strife
That haunt about the ways of life,
Came crying out on Death, that he
Should thus have come so suddenly
To steal the little life away
That would have been so sweet a prey.

'Nay rest thee darling,' then said I,
'Surely 't is better far to lie
Asleep with Death, if God so please,
Than walk with shadows such as these!'

PÆAN.

SING Pæan for the rescued one,
    Come sing it soft and low,
Kiss the pale lips of endless peace,
    And bid farewell and go.

He will not feel the burning tears,
    He will not hear the psalm,
His cold feet touch the silent land,
    The stillness and the calm.

He will not tread the way of pain
    Our weary feet have worn,
The way of fear, by which we go
    To meet him at the bourne.

We walk through perils dark and strange,
    And stumble as we go,
We see, and do, and suffer wrong
    That he will never know.

Sing pæan, and bring wood-flowers wild
  To lay upon his breast,
And softly bear our loved one home
  Where loves and sorrows rest.

Sing for his ransom and release
  From mortal fear and fate,
A pæan of eternal peace,
  And bid farewell and wait.

A MIGHT-HAVE-BEEN.

I SAW an old man, thin and grey,
   Who sat like a shadow beside the way:
His eyes were the saddest that ever were seen.
I said, "What dost thou here, my friend?"
"I am thinking," he said, " of a Might-have-been,
And waiting here for the end."

"Hast thou nothing to do, old man," said I,
"I have nothing to do," he said, "but die."
"Hast thou nothing to love?" You should
      have seen
His eyes, as he answered me, "My friend,
My love was only a Might-have-been,
And here I wait for the end."

'TWAS SUNSHINE STILL WITH THEE.

TEN years—bright years—around our feet
    Thy feet have wandered free,
And howsoever dark our path,
    'T was sunshine still with thee.

A little spot of light—thy life—
    Those dark days did enfold
Whose shadows, though they touched thy head,
    Dimmed not its sheen of gold:

A little flower, that in the time
    Of the cold winds we cherished;
Our sad hearts then were glad—and yet
    'T was all that had not perished:

A chord that once made music sweet,
    With chords of answering tone,
And, now that they are silent, sings
    Its melody alone:

Such hast thou seemed, so sweet, so bright,
  So happy heretofore;
And such if thou might'st ever be,
  We would not ask for more.

We love thee for thy happiness,
  We love thy joy to share,
We love thee for thy soft, brown eyes
  And for thy shining hair.

We love thee, love, for all thou art,
  And hast been in the past;
We love thee for thy love, and shall,
  While love and life may last.

And for another love—that lies
  With silence and a pall—
For that poor, buried might-have-been
  We love thee more than all!

Our prayers availed not then—Ah, love,
  Thine eyes are very fair!
And in their orbs I see a light
  That laughs at my despair.

So, though my song may seem too sad,
   It shall not end in sorrow,—
Hope smiles at me from thy dear face,
   With such a bright good-morrow.

THE LOCKET.

THAT wither'd leaf in the locket,
   That leaf of a wither'd flower,
Now dead, and dry, and scentless,
   Hath still a marvellous power:

It brings a day that is dark
   Into the light once more,
And a sad, sweet smile on a face
   That is lingering at the door:

It makes the long, long past
   Seem present, and close, and warm ;—
That wither'd leaf in the locket,
   Carried about like a charm!

A DREAM OF THE PAST.

FROM the noise of the strife, from the battle
    of life,
  I turn, through the desolate years,
To the church of the vow that is holier now,
  For the love that is hallowed by tears.

To live in the faith that is faithful to death,
  We vowed at the altar divine,
And still, as I kneel in the spirit, I feel
  A hand that is resting in mine.

A moment—no more—and the vision is o'er,
  The dream of the past and the tears :
To the noise of the strife, to the battle of life,
  I turn, from the desolate years.

THE TRUMPETS ARE SOUNDING.

THE trumpets are sounding, the heroes are
    falling,
Fighting and falling, foeman and friend,
Let us go up to the front with the foremost,
    Let us go faithfully on to the end.

Fighting or falling, victor or vanquished,
    Still the war goes gallantly by,
You who are shouting the noisy pæans
    Are but waiting your turn to die.

Each to his place in the hour of danger,
    Each in his place to stand or fall,
Asking no question when, or wherefore,
    Each to be ready —and that is all.

Some on the lonely hill-top looking
    Wearily out in the twilight dim,
Some in the thick of the battle bleeding,
    Crushed and broken in life and limb.

All around is the noise of the striving,
    Fierce, harsh voices and dying wails,
Not for pity may any spare thee,
    Only the strength of the strong avails.

Well for thee, if friends are near thee,
    Loving and helping all they can ;
Well for thee, though foes are round thee,
    If thou can'st do and die like a man.

Not for thy life thy life was given,
    But to be spent in the strife of souls;
One way there is to the gates of heaven,
    And o'er it the tumult of conflict rolls.

The trumpets are sounding, the heroes are falling,
    Fighting and falling, foeman and friend,
Let us go up to the front with the brave ones,
    Let us go faithfully on to the end.

A REQUIEM.

"He must not float upon his watery bier unwept."
—*Lycidas.*

LONG before the limbs are weary,
    Long before the day is done,
Or the eyes are dim with gazing
    On the glory of the sun;

Ere the heart has felt a burden,
    Ere the feet have found a snare,
Ere the light of hope had left him
    Walking in the shadow—care;

While the pathways of his being
    Lay before him, stretching far
Underneath the noonday brightness,
    Underneath the evening star;

As the friendly faces greet him,
  As the friendly voices cheer,
As the gladness of the tumult
  Rings like music in his ear;

Even then the shadow passes,
  Even then the darkness falls—
Like a sudden trumpet pealing,
  Even then the angel calls!

He has heard it and is silent,
  And a smile is on his cheek,
And upon his lips the burden
  Of the words he may not speak.

Strange should come to him the message
  For which others watch and pray,
Bowed beneath a weight of sorrow,
  Weary of the night and day!

Strange that eyes so bright with promise
  Should be now so dark with sleep!
Stranger still they should not answer
  To the tears of those who weep!

What is this, that we should murmur?
　　What is this that we should groan?
Do the dead know any sorrow?
　　Do the mute lips ever moan?

Life! Has life so sweet a slumber?
　　Seems he not supremely blest,
Having found what we are seeking—
　　Rest? Nay, something more than rest!

A MEETING.

Written on hearing that R. W. Emerson was coming to England, 1873.

WITHIN a quiet homestead far away
    Sat a lone wight who to himself did say:—
The brave American is coming here,
My prophet of the western hemisphere;
Coming to England, to the holy land
Which Shakspere, Cromwell, Milton made so grand
To all the ages. Taking down his book,
I turn its treasured pages o'er and look
For the old texts, the precious sayings there,
And read, and read again, and breathe a prayer,
That I might see this man, this Emerson;
Or, if high God would grant so great a boon,
Carlyle and him together when they meet.
Seldom in this world do such voices greet,

Whose trumpet tones have rung so clear and high,
Proclaiming man's immortal destiny,
Proclaiming that God's truth is not a lie
For priests to conjure with, that still His word,
If the soul will but listen, may be heard
Within the soul, and from the lips of men,
His prophets, whom He sendeth once again,
And still again will send, till man is freed
From bondage to a dark and soulless creed,
From bondage to a blind and brute despair,
That seeth not the Presence everywhere,
In which we walk unweeting! Oh, ye two,
Who still bear witness that this truth is true,
That howsoever high the heavens appear,
The spirit of the Living God is near
To every soul of man, 't were grand to see
That meeting, and in reverent mood to be
Partakers of its high communion.

But what is this? Have I not seen and known
The truths ye teach, the vision ye have shown?
And in the presence of the Allgood, the Allfair,
Have I not met—shall I not meet you THERE!

BENISON.

A BENISON be thine, true heart,
    Who came true hearts to bless,
A pledge of love for all thy love,
    And all thy faithfulness.

BOON.

A BLESSING on the day, my child,
    A benison for thee,
As full of boon as thy dear love
    Has been a boon to me.

AT REST.

THEY lie at rest, the weary ones
    For whom we mourned in days gone by,
Who lived that we might live, and then
    Lay down to die.

They lie at rest, the little ones
Who smiled and prattled at our knees,
And then were seen on earth no more—
    We mourn for these.

But more for those, with hopeless eyes
Who watch and wait for rest, we mourn,
Who live through life a life of pain,
    With patient scorn.

Who wait but that the end may come
That brings to sorrow its surcease,
And pray for death—because they deem
    That death is peace.

For these we mourn until the hour
When God shall grant their poor request,
And weary with the weary ones
    They lie at rest.

IF I REMEMBER.

IF I remember the beautiful face,
   If still they haunt me, the soft, dark eyes,
The gentle greeting, the gentle smile,
   What then must be thy memories,
Part of whose life has passed away
   With her who hand in hand with thee
Wandered together where life's brief day
   Dawns in the fields of our infancy?

If I regret that these can fill
   No more with their beauty a fleeting hour,
That the lips of love have been kissed by death,
   And the soft lids closed like a frozen flower—
What then to thee, to whom those eyes
   Were part of the light of every morrow,
Is the shadow now on thy path that lies
   That was not always a path of sorrow?

IF I REMEMBER.

If I remember, can'st thou forget
    The days before that shadow fell,
When love, and beauty, and joy were hers,
    And hope was with thee, and all was well?
Yet the path of thy future may be as bright
    With the brightness of hope as it was before,
And love, and beauty, and all delight
    —If thou could'st remember the past no more!

CLEOPATRA.

—

Suggested by a painting attributed to Michael Angelo

THE revels are ended,
   The glory is fled,
The voices are silent
   And Antony—dead !

O Charmian, O Iras,
   The darkness is come,
The dancers are weary,
   The music is dumb.

The gods give to Cæsar
   The world and its powers,
But love and the triumph
   Of love has been ours.

The mouth of the serpent
  Of Nile at my breast
Is sweet as thy kisses
  To kiss me to rest.

And softer than slumber
  On love-weary eyes,
When wan day is dying,
  This death-shadow lies.

The vanquished is victor,
  The captive is free—
Octavius will triumph,
  But not over me!

A QUESTION OF IMMORTALITY.

To one who sneeringly doubted his own.

ASKEST me, art thou immortal?
    I neither know nor care.
I only know the soul's immortal,
And cometh everywhere.

Ask thy soul, man, if thou hast one,
    And cease thy foolish quest.
Thou art not sure thou hast one? Well –
Thou'rt likely to know best!

LOCH ACHRAY.[2]
MAY 20, 1877.

AN old, familiar scene,
    This little mountain mere,
These woods to me have been,
    For many a silent year;

A picture in a room,
    A glimpse of sun and shade,
Brown heath and forest gloom,
    By painter's pencil made;

A dream of summer skies
    On Highland peaks unknown,
A rest for weary eyes
    That wait and watch alone;

A dream, a name—no more,—
    Till this fair morn of spring
Upon the sylvan shore
    I hear the mavis sing:

LOCH ACHRAY.

Music is in the brake
    And sunshine in the trees,
And my enchanted lake
    Is rippling in the breeze!

I tread the daisied grass,
    And by the mossy burn
I wander up the pass,
    Among the budding fern :

By peak and plain I stray,
    I leave the lonely glen,
I take my homeward way,
    Ne'er to return again.

The wild wood-bird will sing
    Under the mountain hoar,
And gentle winds will bring
    The ripple to the shore ;

But not a voice to me
    Will come from lake or hill,
No music from the tree,
    No murmur from the rill.

So little I bring home
   To what I had before ;—
A picture in my room,
   A name—a dream :—no more!

DALMALLY.

"Ay, now am I in Arden; the more fool I, when I was at home I was in a better place. But travellers must be content."
As You Like It.

OH, grand are the hills looking over Dalmally,
    And green are the forests and fair,
And tranquil the streams that run down in the valley,
    And lovely the flowers that grow there!

And there by the way-side the tavern is cozy,
    Inviting the stranger to stay,
And there is the waiter who bringeth 'the rosy,'
    And there is the bill you've to pay.

There, foot-worn and weary, you rest from your roaming,
    Who come with no cares but your own,
You quietly puff your cigar in the gloaming,
    And tipple your toddy alone.

But if you come there with a comrade unquiet,
  Who grumbles and growls at his lot,
Who turns up the tip of his nose at the diet,
  And findeth no peace in the pot;

For you will no rest be, though never so weary,
  No 'ease at your inn' will you find;
The vale will be dark and the hills will be dreary,
  And dismal the state of your mind.

And should you come there with a couple of franions
  Who quarrel like dogs o'er a bone,
It's fifty to one you will curse your companions,
  And wish you had come there alone.

For, grand though the hills be that look o'er Dalmally,
  And green though the forests and fair,
If with quarrelsome cronies you come to the valley,
  You may have a 'row' even there!

And you who seek peace among mountains and flowers,
  Wherever your footsteps may roam,
You'll seek it in vain in the happiest bowers—
  If you set off without it from home.

A TRUE FORGETMENOT.

I 'VE roamed thro' woods and meadows wide,
   I've wandered oft in gardens gay,
And many a lovely flower I've seen,
   And gather'd many a sweet bouquet.

Red is the rose and sometimes white,
   The lily like the snow new driven,
And in the tulip may be seen
   All colours of the bow of heaven.

Sweet is the briar, whose name is sweet,
   And sweet also the violet,
And thyme, and mint, and marjoram,
   And wall-flower and the mignonette.

But not a flower in all the world
   Can match in beauty or in bloom
This paragon of Flora's art :—
   Its rounded grace—its soft perfume !

A TRUE FORGETMENOT.

I ask not that the red, red rose
   Or snow-white lily be my dower—
All that I dared not ask I have,
   In this my cream-white cauliflower.

Thanks, lady, for the souvenir,
   Thrice happy in whose humble pot
Descends the culinary flower,
   The only true Forgetmenot!

A QUARTETTE. [3]

Written in a Lady's Album

WITHIN this little book
　　Immortal lines you read,
By your most famous wights,
　For wit and daring deed.

A journey, all on foot,
　To famous London city
Has proved how brave they are,—
　These pages prove how witty.

The Duke can soar aloft
　In verse sublime and strong,
Or stoop to mushrooms, when he lists
　"'To check the vein of song."

The General cannot soar,
  His heels no pinions bear,
For once sharp fate, as Hamlet says,
  Did "set a blister there."

The gay Lieutenant next
  Comes briskly to the fore,
Whose merry jests have often set
  The table in a roar.

Mine Ancient jesteth not—
  A silent sort of man—
Yet thus to please a fair ladye
  He does the best he can.

A BIRTHDAY-RHYME.

YES, the weather's very cold, and the Muse is very mournful,
And the "Duke" you may be sure, would be very, very scornful,
If I were to compose a verse or two in prose,
With a tinkle at the endings that everybody knows—
Because he could do it better, or his Muse, if he would let her,
Although it is a task that he does not often set her.
And though for "friends to part" is a sadness to the heart,
Yet, as vulgar folk would say, it is quite another start,
When old chums meet together, who have seen a deal of weather,
And worn a deal of leather, a-roaming o'er the heather,
To talk of good old has-been, and sit and puff their smoke,
And unearth the dismal pun and the venerable joke:

And sure 't would be a pity, if the muse so wise
  and witty,
Couldn't find it in her heart to sing a random
  ditty :
And the bard, if such a bard there be, would be
  a ninny,
If he could not tune his precious pipes and turn
  a rhyme for Minnie,
On a high day such as this is, and wish a thousand
  blisses,
All good that life possesses, and a wealth of
  household kisses,
For the maiden young and fair, and the mother
  debonair,
And the "General" a-sitting in his old arm
  chair.
So here's honour to the day, to the lassie bright
  and gay,
Be her's the true heart-gladness that will never
  pass away.
May the summer of her life be as cloudless as
  the spring,
May sorrow never touch her with its dark and
  heavy wing.
So prays "mine Ancient" and the rest will join
  him in his prayer,
The "Duke" and the "Lieutenant," and also
  the ex-Mayor :
Here's to your health and happiness ! and when
  the toast is done,
Let's hope the merry alderman will crown it with
  a pun.

ON A CERTAIN POEM,[4]

Published in a certain paper, without the knowledge or consent of the Editor.

WHAT'S this, ye auld "sneck-drawing dog?"
    Behind my chair you " came incog,
And played on me a cursed brogue,
    Black be your fa' "—
And gave my dignity " a shog,
    'Maist ruined a'."

I'm not so fain as you might think
To answer you with pen and ink,
Or file and fashion, link by link,
    An idle rhyme ;
It may be I'm too near the brink
    And bourne of time.

And there are other reasons why
"My Muse," as you say "is so shy,"
We'll talk them over by and bye
   Before the end,
Before the days have all gone by,
   My trusty friend.

Let us be thankful we have known
The Muse at all, in this dark zone
Of factory-fumes, this Acheron
   Of soot and sin ;
That we *have* tasted pure ozone,
   Parnassian !

You've had your Burns, you have him still ;
I have my Shakespeare, my sweet Will ;
Pure fountains from the heavenly hill,
   And blest are they
Who of such waters drink their fill
   In life's brief day.

"The Editorial chair is hard ?"—
Well, it's not just a throne, my Bard,
But while it wins some small regard
   Fra' chiels like you,
I take it kindly, as reward
   For service due.

Both you and I have sat on stools
Of harder wood, with harder tools
Than pen or pencil: in such schools,
 The truth to tell,
Without much aid of bookish rules,
 We learned to spell.

We learned to read, we learned the song
The Muses sing; we learned ere long
The sacred lore of right and wrong;
 We did abide
The battle where the foe was strong;
 We took our side;

We fought together. Let it go.
You make no brag of that, I know;
Patient you bore the dastard blow,
 With cheer sublime,
Then turned on the retreating foe
 "A routh o' rhyme."

And still you sing your songs of cheer,
You care not though the critics sneer.
Why should you? Humble souls sincere
 Accept the lay:
You pipe away from year to year,
 A minstrel gay.

ON A CERTAIN POEM.

So should it be, my festive spark;
We never weary of the lark,
And in this world of care and cark
    We need your gladness,
For sure the world is all too dark
    For songs of sadness.

And mine were sad, and sad enough,
Oh, very melancholy stuff,
A farthing rushlight in the snuff,
    By sorrow tended,
Till in the socket with a puff
    'T was fitly ended.

But sad or glad, my trusty frere
We've been good friends for many a year,
And with a "frater feeling" dear,
    United still,
We'll gather in some far off sphere,
    Wi' Rab and Will!

A SILVER WEDDING.

How swift time flies on silver wings
   To the silver wedding-day,
How silver sweet the time-voice sings
   Upon that silver way.

How happy they, with silver crown
   Who crown the happy years,
Where from the hill-top looking down
   Another dawn appears.

Another dawn, a restful time,
   And restful be the way,
By which you "toddle down" the hill
   To the "golden" wedding day.

"Entire affection" speedeth time,
   But time is never old
To those he brings on silver wings
   Into the years of gold.

Another dawn will yet arise,
    For mornings never cease ;
And close upon the evening time
    Will come the dawn of peace.

A MEMORY

Of Edmund Spenser and George Fox.

———

I PASSED through wonderful valleys
  Where wealth had built its towers,
Where din of crank and wheel was heard
  Through all the sun-bright hours;

Where busy men were scheming
  In dim and dusty rooms,
And simple folk were moiling
  All day in the deafening looms:

And in the stony roadways,
  Where crowding feet would come,
I heard the mingling echoes,
  The clash and clamour, and hum:

A MEMORY.

And all above the valleys
    A dismal cloud hung low,
Poisoning the rain, and sunshine,
    And all sweet winds that blow :

And I saw in all men's faces
    One craft of a cunning brain,
In all men's voices I heard one speech
    Whose sweetest word was 'gain.'

There was but one dream in every mind,
    In every heart one care—
And few had thought of the sunshine
    That lives in the summer air.

And few had thought for the mystic gleam
    That kindles the poet's rhyme,
That burns in the prophet's burning prayer
    Through all the night of time.

And I asked an ancient moiler,
    As he walked beside me there,
If ever he heard a poet's song
    Or the voice of a prophet's prayer.

And he said he heard the parson
    Of the parish once-a-week,
But for bard or prophet, wellaway,
    Of them he could not speak.

And I asked if no wandering minstrel
    Through the valleys ever trod,
And if never had stood on the glorious hills
    The feet of a knight of God.

And the moiler stared with puzzled look
    And ne'er a word would he say,
But I saw the scorn in his cunning eye
    As he laughed and walked away.

Then I turned again through the roadways
    And sought in a dusty nook,
Where, under the frowning gables,
    Was many an ancient book ;

And there I read of a minstrel,
    A bard of the olden time,
Who in these valleys nursed his youth
    And planned his glorious rhyme ;

And there I read of a wandering seer,
    A prophet of the soul,
Whose prayer went up from yonder hill
    That looks towards the pole :

And I mused, as the crowd went by me,
    If one poor moiler there
Had heard of that minstrel's wondrous song,
    Or that old prophet's prayer.

A CENOTAPH.

APRIL 23RD, 1864.

What needs my Shakespeare for his honour'd bones
The labour of an age in pilèd stones,
Or that his hallow'd relics should be hid
Under a star-y-pointing pyramid.
Dear son of Memory, great heir of Fame,
What need'st thou such weak witness of thy name?
Thou in our wonder and astonishment
Hast built thyself a live-long monument ;
. . . .
And so sepulcred in such pomp doth lie
That kings for such a tomb would wish to die.

— *Milton.*

WITH happy radiance rose this April morn,
  Three hundred years ago,
When, on the banks of that delightful stream —
The willowy Avon, that with whispering flow
Now creeps through woodland shadows, now
  doth glow

Bright in the sun among the meadow flowers,
Now glassing in its depths some pastoral scene,
And now reflecting Warwick's feudal towers ;
There where the humble village spire doth stand
To which the pilgrims turn from every land ;
There in the quiet, cool, auspicious hours,
While nature robed the earth in freshest green,
 Shakespeare was born.
And there his infancy was nursed, and there
 With flowers his childhood played ;
And through the leafy lanes and meadows fair
 A glorious boy he strayed.
And there in youthful sport the woodlands hoary
He roamed with each bold spirit of the time,
Who, like the shepherds of the ancient story,
'Mongst whom Apollo came with veilèd glory,
Knew not the godhead of that brow sublime.
And there a man he lived, and night and day
Visited him in their sweet, alternate sway ;
 And there he died :
 And there his tomb is found :
And that low spot of earth is more renowned
Than all the monuments of human pride.

In temples reared by any mortal hand
Do we his mighty Cenotaph behold?

Among the tombs of princes doth it stand,
    In marble or in gold ?
Ah, no ! but in the temple of the mind,
Upreared sublime, by his own genius wrought,
His monumental effigies we find,
Enduring with the eternities of thought !
No sacerdotal gloom around it lowers,
No night of ignorance ever darkens there,
Where in the light of nature upward towers
    That structure fair.
And Nature owns it ; Nature on it showers
The sunlight of her own eternities :
" The pyramids of man are dust," she cries,
" But this is mine ; and with my work shall bear
An equal rank, even with my stars and flowers."

Low on its adamantine base around
Are fiendish shapes and aspects of the earth :
There brutal Caliban, of monstrous birth,
Grovels beneath his torturers on the ground :
    There the pale Hecat's crew
    Their fatal poisons brew :
There open-eyed conspirators are seen
    In whispering talk ;
There lust, and cruelty, and hate, and fear,
    Cunning, and treachery, appear ;
    There madness mopes and raves ;

There the blood-boltered ghosts of murdered men
    Rise from untimely graves.

And next in place are all the aspects shown
Of human folly, from the Athenian boor,
With ass's head and ears, through knave and
    clown,
Now to the verge of idiotcy down,
Now upward ranging to the feathery brain
Of nimble-witted foppery. Never sure
Was foolery writ on any face so plain
As upon these; save some that we have known.
And never shall we see such fools again
As we have met in Arden many a day,
    Sicilia's Court, or in Illyria,
Denmark, or where the towers of Venice rise.
    Yet these and more are there,
Who mingled much of wisdom with their jest:
    And in his tavern chair,
Falstaff, so fat, so witty, and so wise,
    Sits high above the rest.

And after these, as by enchantment wrought,
The enchanted isle, full of all sweetest sound,
And Ariel's song echoing the rocks around,
And coral-bedded seas, by magic taught
    Along the haunted shore
      To heave, and dash, and roar.

And fairy-land with all its bowers of green,
　　And Oberon's court is seen,
　　And that fair Indian child,
Titania's train, and all the revels wild
　　Held on the moonlit sward ;
And Theseus in the woods of Attica,
　　Hunting the boar and pard.
And here, behold, a shepherd's holiday,
With Florizel, and Perdita the fair
Weaving her garlands of immortal flowers.
　　There, breathing tranquil air,
Are those who dwell in Arden's peaceful bowers,
　　Fleeting the happy hours
Beneath the shadows of the forest old,
　　As in the age of gold.

And over these the stately forms are seen
　　Of kings with royal mein ;
　　Heroes and statesmen old,
And forms sublime of Greek and Roman mould;
The Trojan warrior and his Grecian foe,
Ulysses' thoughtful eyes and Nestor's locks of
　　snow :
Coriolanus, haughty, brave, austere ;
Cassius and Brutus, patriot souls severe ;
Imperial Cæsar, fearless, calm and wise ;
Marc Antony, who forfeited the prize
Of Rome and empire for the Egyptian's eyes.

And next in order, see,
The knightly race of English chivalry ;
Harry the king, Bedford and Exeter,
Warwick and Salisbury, Suffolk, York, are there,
Whose names are household words, and many
    more
Who fought with them that day at Agincourt,
And after, when the white rose and the red
Heaped many an English field high with the
    noble dead.

And, lo, a matchless sight !
Like some "entire and perfect chrysolite"
Of sculptured loveliness is yon fair band ;
Beauty and pleasure, breathing happy breath
" Beauty and anguish, walking hand in hand
    The downward way to death."
Lo, Beatrice, with flashing wit and eyes ;
Hero's mute woe ; Miranda's glad surprise ;
Imogene's truth ; Viola's patient sighs ;
Sweet Rosalind, and gentle Celia ;
The lovely lady, " married to the Moor :"
Sad Isabel, Hermione, and poor
    Love-crazed Ophelia ;
And, see, a radiance from the portal breaks
Of yonder tomb, that opens on the night,
" For there lies Juliet, and her beauty makes
That vault a feasting presence, full of light !"

>   High over these again,
> Crowning with glory all that work sublime,
>   Stand the colossal men
> Who strove with fate, and passion, and the blind
> Furies whose haunts are in the human mind;
> Majestic forms, enduring to all time;
> Timon, that soul of fierce Titanic hate
> Whose curses fall like oracles of fate.
> Shylock, the stubborn and unpitying Jew;
> That Hunchback who the sleeping princes slew;
> The Moor, so loving, jealous, cruel, kind;
> Macbeth, who murdered sleep; and she whose
>   form
> Still walks beside him like a fate; and blind
> Old Lear, whose awful grief outstorms the storm;
> Romeo, poor Juliet's heavenly Romeo,
> The immortal minion of love and woe;
> And he, as madness wild, as wisdom sane,
> As nature's self profound—Hamlet the Dane!

> What monument was ever yet designed,
> Wrought out of nature or the human mind;
> What pyramids, or parthenons, or domes;
> What palace towers, what gorgeous abbey-glooms;
> What Phidian grace to Grecian marbles given;
> What Titian hues, what Raphael dreams of
>   heaven;

What pomp of mingling harmonies, that roll
Their waves of rapture through the listening soul!
Of the poetic muse, what legends fine,
Homeric gods or heroes half divine ;
Dantean terrors of the gulf profound,
Or mystic lights that star the godhead round :
Miltonic wars, where giant angels fight
Or fall with ruin from the plains of light ;
What work of genius, wrought with highest aim,
And consecrate to everlasting fame,
  Can match with this that bears our wisest
    Shakespeare's name ?

A RHYME OF JUBILEE. [7]
JANUARY 1883.

A LITTLE stream began to flow
Among the wild hills long ago,
A little well which hands of toil
Had scooped out of the barren soil,
And two or three who thirsted there
Drank of the waters sweet and fair,
Drank as they rested from the strain
Of nervous hand and busy brain,
Drank and were glad, as men who find,
Wandering in deserts lone and blind,
A little nook of wild fern growing,
Whereby a blessed fount is flowing.

Or say, a little seed was sown,
Where erst the summer flowers had grown
In meadows to our fathers known ;

"The Meadows," as we still must say,
Although no grass grows there to-day,
But there this seed was scattered then,
By faithful hands of humble men,
Whose flowers to-day are gathered far,
Wherever faithful toilers are;
Flowers fairer than were ever seen
On lonely hills, in valleys green,
And lovelier fruit than that whose gold
Was guarded by the dragon old;
And this grows free for all to eat,
"The best of Pan's immortal meat,"
So sweet is thought, and knowledge sweet.

Or say, a little light alone
Out of a cottage window shone,
At first a thin and trembling ray
Shot through the night-mist dim and grey,
And two or three with wondering eyes
Saw the soft light and watched it rise,
And like a beacon burn afar,
Until the lamp became a star!
A star that blesses humble ways,
That hallows toil and toilsome days;
And thousands follow now that light,
Who walked in peril of the night

Of ignorance, so blind and drear,
Where myriads perish in their fear.

Lo, now, where'er the poor man turns
That glorious light around him burns,
Which poor men kindled long ago.

Lo, now, the flowers that round us blow,
The plantings of a poor man's care,
Make all our pathways sweet and fair.

Lo, now, a river, wide and grand,
Upon whose banks ten thousands stand,
And those who pass from land to land.
Is this the little well that burst
Up in "The Meadows," scarce at first
Enough for those poor men athirst!

So speak we of beginnings old,
Dark years that into bright years rolled
And brought us what we have.—Behold!
"Look round;" so still it must be said
To those who ask about the dead,
Who did good work that must endure,
Who laid the strong foundations sure.

A RHYME OF JUBILEE. 187

What need I tell to those who know—
You who have seen the long years go,
Who saw the little done before
Still added to the little more?
And you who stand as in the prime
And promise of a happier time,
"Look round you," so I still must say,
You children of the coming day,
Look round with proud and happy glance
At all your fair inheritance.
What have you here? Light, learning, store
Of gathered science, and the lore
Of ages past—art—poetry—
And more, for more than these must be—
The perfect freedom of the free.
For what is knowledge but a chain,
A burden upon heart and brain,
To men afraid of liberty.
For this our fathers fought of old,
Right faithful men were they and bold,
Right faithful, too, the men who stood
Together, working for our good,
And watching, amid doubts and fears,
The slow results of fifty years.
The men who added stone to stone,
Who built what now is all our own,
Who added book to book, and brought

The hoarded wealth of human thought,
And teachers wise, and day by day
Laboured themselves, till they were grey,
Laboured, and taught, and passed away.
Shall we not own the mighty debt?
Shall we these faithful men forget,
Now that we crown the work they did?
Honour and gratitude forbid!
Here in this temple where we stand
Shall we not praise the building hand?
Shall we not bless the head that planned?
Shall we not name the honoured name?
Shall we not give the giver fame?

Look through the mist of fifty years,
And, lo, the gentle face appears
Of Thomas Booth; I see him stand,
A leader in the little band
Who laid the first foundations down
Of that great edifice we crown.

Who next out of the darkened days
Answers our proud appeal of praise?
A faithful worker, kind and strong,
Who laboured earnestly and long,
With free good will. Methinks, I hear
A voice out of the past ring clear—

A RHYME OF JUBILEE.

"When you have built a house," said one,
"And fair to look at in the sun,
Worthy this cause so good and grand,
Oh, leave a niche for Sutherland!"
Although that niche is empty yet,
Not here, not now, must we forget
The name of one who wrought so well.

Yet of another let me tell,
Who did good work that will endure,
Who knew the rede of science pure,
Who taught and loved the legends old
That round the rustic hearth are told,
And linger on the haunted wold;
Who called again the ghosts of war
To lift the lance and urge the oar
Along the banks of lonely Brun :
For all this faithful labour done,
How much we owe to Wilkinson.

How much to these, how much to thee,
The friend of light and liberty,
Who trusted truth to make men free ;
The faithful life, the generous hand,
The kind good heart, the head that planned,
In its benevolence sublime,
Large blessings for the coming time,

Whose generations here shall turn,
Long as the lamps of science burn,
To gladden many a humble lot,
While thousands bless the name of Scott.

Another name I have to name
Of those who wrought nor thought of fame,
Of those who did the cause befriend,
Who knew the work, but not the end ;
Good men, and true, and strong, were they ;
And he who left us yesterday,
Was he not strong—was he not wise—
The man whose memory we prize
Before all others for the light
He made around him in the fight ?
For in that time of fifty years
Did we not strive with doubts and fears,
With hollow friends and bitter foes ?
And when the angry zealots rose
To rend in twain our peaceful band,
How strong and fearless did he stand,
Whose voice was still a voice of power,
Whose very presence was a tower,
Built firm on simple rectitude :
And for a sure and solid good,
If any work to him did seem,
He would not leave it for a dream.

Some say the wisest of the wise
Are they who see what nearest lies
About their feet, nor go astray,
Nor ever stumble by the way;
Of such was he. You know the name,
You know the record without blame
Of William Miller Coultate, when
Shall we behold his like again.

These for the old time's sake we name.
There may be some with equal claim
We name not, men content to know
The work was good and let it go,
Content to know it will not die.
So wrought they in the years gone by;
And so we crown their work and say,
Well done! But is it finished? Nay,
Each willing worker of to-day
Will say, the work is but begun;
Ask Brumwell, Greenwood, Anningson,
Ask Thompson, Colbran, Foden, too,
That faithful worker, tried and true;
And you—if I appeal to you—
Is there one free and generous heart
Not ready from this day to start
Upon another fifty years?
For if in darkness, doubts, and fears,

The little seed by poor men sown
To all these grand results has grown,
Shall you, who look with hope before,
Not take good courage to do more?

The good work done has been well done ;
The work to do is well begun ;
Out of the past a little light ;
And in the future prospects bright
And goodly, opening far away
The promise of a perfect day !

Behold! the night and morning meet ;
Behold ! the past and future greet ;
And young and old rejoice to see
This glad and solemn Jubilee !

FOR A "PENNY READING."

Given in the Mechanics' Institution, Burnley, in honour of the Marriage of the Princess Royal with Prince Frederick William of Prussia, January 25th, 1858.

IN her high palace, amid pomp and gold,
   Our Queen to-night her festive court doth hold
For her fair daughter, on whose nuptial state,
Grace, beauty, genius, wealth and power do wait,
Her genii of the lamp. She wills—and see,
Around her glows the bright emblazonry!
On every hand heraldic splendours shine,
Hues that the painter's art has made divine,
And sculpture's godlike forms that seem to bless,
With tranquil eyes, her living loveliness.
Rapt poesy upon her state attends,
And the high Tragic Muse unto her bends,

And Comedy, with laughter-lighted face,
Lends to the gorgeous scene her mimic grace,
And the gay spirit of the dance is there,
And music trembling through the perfumed air!
Nor there alone—in many a proud saloon
Will the bright lamps outwatch the waning moon,
And many a stately hall to-night will be
A scene of rare fantastic revelry,
Where youth and beauty meet in festal bands,
Throughout the breadth of these historic lands,
To celebrate a marriage that combines
In happy union two Imperial lines,
While every belfry-tower in honour rings
Of the fair daughter of a hundred kings!

But not to princely domes confined alone
This loyal homage to our ancient throne;
For many a lowlier roof will see to-night
Its festive gathering of faces bright,
In honour of this royal bridal day,
And of our gracious Queen, whose gentle sway
Is a free land's inestimable dower
Of wise restriction and of temperate power;
And though our own among the lowliest be,
Yet may it not the less enjoyment see,
While our poor services to-night we lend,
For your amusement, to this loyal end,

And in rude fashion, on our little stage,
Mimic the humours quaint of youth and age;
Craving your kind indulgence while we strive
Unto imaginary forms to give
Life, motion, voice; and that you still may be
Mindful of this, that in these efforts we—
Though imperfections mar the passing scenes—
Have done our utmost with our little means.

EPILOGUE

Spoken at a Dramatic Performance given in the Theatre Royal, Thursday, January 4th, 1866, under the patronage of Alderman Robinson, Mayor, for the benefit of the Burnley Cricket Club.

ONCE on a time there was an age of steel,
"Ere human statute purged the gentle weal,"
When the strong arm and daring heart alone
Against contending swords could hold its own,
When knaves and fools by force were kept in awe,
When strength and valour were the only law;
Then rough and savage as the times might be,
The hearts of men were full of chivalry,
Then beauty, if the ancient songs say sooth,
Was guarded on its way by knightly truth,
In bower or greenwood ever walked secure
From foul defaming tongue or eyes impure

But times have changed, and wrong and insult now,
If they but wear the sanctimonious brow,
May pass unchallenged, or may even chance
To win the loud acclaim of ignorance.

Behold, where late appeared the matchless grace
Of two fair beings of ethereal race ;
On either's face beauty and genius sit,
And in their eyes the fires of love are lit,
And both are crowned; one with the light supreme
Of poetry and passion's burning dream :
And pleasure's rose and wit's unvalued gem
The other wears—a peerless diadem.
Upon the first attend in awful state
All the dread ministers of human fate,—
Anger, with eyes in their own lightnings blind,
And trembling fear that starts at every wind,
Revenge, with dripping sword, and dumb Despair,
And Horror shrieking with uplifted hair ;
Malignant Envy, and unholy Hate,
And holiest Love is there, on whom doth wait
Sorrow forever like a shadowy fear,
"And Pity dropping soft the sadly pleasing tear."
Around the other dance a festive train,
Lovely as shapes that haunt the poet's brain,—

Mirth, with quick laughter in her voice and eye,
And Fancy crowned with flowers that never die,
Wit, with her sparkling glance and merry wiles,
And the arch Humour, with her softer smiles,
And Cheerfulness with roseate bloom is there,
"And Joy enchanted smiles and waves her
    golden hair!"

Attended thus came those fair sisters, born
Above the reach of ignominious scorn,
Above the reach of foul, calumnious wrong,
And heralded by "music's golden tongue,"
And heralded by many a deathless song.
They came to bless, to elevate, to soothe,
To cheer the weariness of toil, to smooth
The wrinkles on the rugged brow of care,
With fantasies of mirth and visions rare,
With high and innocent pleasures to allure
The wandering steps of youth from ways impure.
'Twas thus they came,— and how were they
    received?
Oh, be it not for very scorn believed!
'Tis true the winning grace, the genial smile,
Drew audience and attention for awhile,
But the first warmth of welcome soon grew cold,
Indifference came, and envious foes, grown
    bold,

From tongue to tongue the whispered slander flew,
And gathering strength and fury as it grew,
Burst in a howl of bigotry and rage
On those twin Muses of the buskined stage,
And Tragedy bowed low her haughty head,
And from her sister's face the roseate smiles have fled.

Who first withstood this rude assault of shame?
Who threw the shelter of his potent name,
Like a strong shield, by knightly hand extended,
O'er beauty innocent and unbefriended?
'Twas he, the first in place, who fills the chair
Of civic dignity, our honoured Mayor.
He o'er fanatic hate awhile prevailed,
And at his presence cant and folly quailed.
But not to one unaided arm we trust
To lay this rabble rout low in the dust,
Let them come on, we will not quail with fear
With such a host as are assembled here.
To you, ye heroes of the bat and ball,
Ye gallant champions of the club, I call;
To you the Tragic and the Comic Muse
Call for assistance, nor will you refuse,
Like knights who sheltered beauty in distress,
Around them here to-night you nobly press.

And swear your bats their best defence will be
Against the tomahawks of bigotry.
Thus shall you gain the favour of the "gods,"
And win your matches 'gainst the mightiest odds,
And thus the Tragic Muse shall cease to mourn,
And all the grace of Comedy return :
For at your presence, lo! they rise again,
And come to honour you with all their train !
You in whose ready help they gladly see
The spirit of the ancient chivalry,
The strength and valour that of old defended
The weak, the beautiful, the unbefriended,
And against brute and bigot force did dare
To shelter all was beautiful and fair.

PROLOGUE

Written for the opening of the winter season at the
Theatre Royal, Burnley, December 3rd, 1866.

ALTHOUGH 't is four long months since last
we met,
Like Hamlet's ghost, we're not forgotten yet.
I see it in the smiling faces round ;
I hear it in the glad, applauding sound.
And now, to own the soft impeachment true—
Neither have we ourselves forgotten you,
And your past favours,—for, although we hear
You can, at times, be very cold, severe,
Unjust, and everything, in fact, alarming,
To us your generosity's quite charming.
I should be glad if anyone could tell
Whether 't is true that we deserve so well ;

Or that your favours on our efforts rest
Only because we always do our best.
However this may be, 'twill not be vain,
As we have pleased, to hope to please again.

"I could a tale unfold,"—but then you will
Prefer, no doubt, to read it in "the bill,"—
Of all that we intend, and if we do it
"Blazes of triumph" will be nothing to it.
But this is boasting, and upon my word,
I did not think of being so absurd;
Because you know so well what we can do
In drama, and burlesque, and ballet too.
If you remember Ariadne's grace,
And the strange gambols of the Satyr race;
If you remember, too, the Widow Twankay,
Aladdin's mother, loving, lean, and lanky;
And, amongst other things, if you have not
A certain "Little Treasure" quite forgot;
And still retain some faint and dim reflection
Of "The Rough Diamond" in your recollection,
You'll give us credit, if for nothing more,
Yet for the power to please you as before.
And granting this, we'll answer for the rest,
As we intend to "better what was best;"
If but to quit the favours you have shown,
And out of simple gratitude alone.

Time was that here the drama had no place,
Save whence it took some tarnish of disgrace:
A wooden building, like a booth or tent,
Where often rather wooden people went
To hear, perhaps, a very wooden play,
With wooden players; mind, I do not say
That this was always so,—sometimes it chanced
That sparks of genuine thought or feeling, glanced
Athwart that wooden gloom, with fitful glare,
And lit all eyes with pleasure even there.
Now, what a transformation in the scene!
Here might the wand of Harlequin have been,
For lo, a little theatre, all gay,
With lights, and music, and the piled array
Of happy faces, where you may enjoy,
Entirely free from all that can annoy
Your finer sense, the drama's wondrous range
Of wit, and thought and passion sweet and strange;
Behold its shining scenes of human life,
Pleased and instructed by the mimic strife;
And learn a lesson higher than the schools
In the good-natured wisdom of its fools.

Now for ourselves. We come, if so you choose,
To give you pleasure—simply to amuse.
Our only aim and purpose is in this,—

"We are no orators, as Brutus is."
By this I mean, of course, we do not preach;
Such things are quite beyond our utmost reach.
We only seek to tickle you with laughter,
Or draw a tear, perhaps, the moment after.
If we beguile an hour or two away,
After the anxious labours of the day,—
If at our bidding sorrow's eye undims,
And toil relaxes all his weary limbs,—
If we can smooth away one wrinkle there,
Upon that brow so deeply lined with care;
If we can give the rude, uncultured mind
Some newer thought, some feeling more refined;
If we can dimple innocence with smiles,
And make even guilt forget its own deep wiles;
If we can add one pleasure to the day,
Or charm one trouble from the heart away,
It is enough—we seek to do no more
Than, let us hope, we oft have done before.

And if we can amuse without offence
To nature, virtue, truth, or innocence,
We can do much—for, take it as a rule,
To do this well, you must not be a fool.

Yet more than this has oft been done, they say,
With "guilty creatures sitting at the play."

At least, I think you've heard of such a thing,
How once it caught "the conscience of a king."
To these high issues we make no pretence;
'T is true that in our most extravagance
We follow nature, who to our surprise,
Finds even in folly wisdom for the wise.
For those who cannot see it, there's no way
But to enjoy the fun as best they may.
Should you do that, it matters little here,
If you're a fool or a philosopher.
Be merry and wise, too, if you can be so,
But still be merry whether wise or no;
So may we for your liberal favours call,
And wish a "merry Christmas" to you all.

FOR A HOUSE OF HEALING.

Prologue read at an Amateur Dramatic Performance given in the Mechanics' Institution for the benefit of the Victoria Hospital, February, 1886.

THE world is but a stage—you know the saying—
A stage where every man some part is playing.
As here between the wings the actors make
Their entrances, and there their exit take,
So on the wings of time, for time hath wings,
On which he flies, as every poet sings,
Life's pageant passes, beggars, cads and kings.
Men are but mouthing players, says Macbeth,
The heroes of an hour of mortal breath,
Mere walking shadows, and they come and go
Much like the figures in a puppet-show.
Even so, we say, life passes, so it ends,
As when the curtain on a play descends.

And if the world be but a stage, what then?
Is life not real, are the men not men?
Is pain not true, and human suffering?
And heartache, is there really no such thing?
And if pain's real, is not pleasure so?
Is there no difference between weal and woe,
Between the comfort and the rich man's gold
And homeless want that shivers in the cold?
All these are not less real, though we say
They're but the shows and pageants of a play.
What's real, what's unreal, who can know?
The hoarded treasure melts away like snow,
Though barred and buried in a brazen tower,
And guarded strong by all the thrones of power.
What's real? Empires fall and pass away,
But the deep thought of old is ours to-day,
And love and pity will not know decay,
Though love and pity live but in a play.
The world's a stage: why then the world should be
Almost as real as Antigone,
As real as the tears Cordelia shed,
Or Lear's that burn and "scald like molten lead."
The world's a stage : why then the world's as true
As Hamlet is, as sweet with morning dew
As Arden was, when Rosalind lived there
And jested with Orlando, and as fair
As that Italian garden, hushed and trim,

Where the wan lilies and the violet's dim
Trembled to hear the sound of Romeo's feet
And Juliet's voice of love, so " silver sweet."

But such a stage as that would scarce be real,
You'll say, or what then shall we call ideal,
If these are not so? Call them what you please,
They touch, they charm, they give us calm and ease,
And pleasure pure; they help us as we go
Upon a weary way; could they do so
Were they less real than the world we know?

The ideal then is real, shall we say,
In life itself and in the life-like play?
They are, at any rate, so near allied,
We ever meet them going side by side,
As through the fairy forests, white as snow,
The gentle Una with St. George did go;
And as these helped each other by the way
With counsel and with comfort, so do they.

Life is a battle—but the Redcross goes
With Una by his side against his foes;
Life is a battle—but Cordelia bright
Moves through the tumult like a shape of light.
As in the play, so is it in the world,
Where the red flag of war has been unfurled,
There shall we see the white-cross banner flying,
There pity helps the wounded and the dying.

In the Greek play, among the warrior dead,
Antigone, by heavenly pity led,
Went forth alone ; but now where foe meets foe
To every battlefield a thousand go
On the same errand, with as pure intent,
As that on which the high-souled Theban went.
Thus pity helps the world, a fair ideal,
And the play helps to make that pity real,
And thus the play would help us still, if we
Could make it worthy of humanity,
As Shakespeare did, and even, be it said,
With all its faults and sins upon its head,
The play still helps the world, and brightens it
With pleasant fancies, feeling, sense and wit,
And makes the burden easier to bear
Of mortal suffering and human care.
The world's a battle field, but not alone
Where the gun thunders and the trumpet's blown;
In every house and home, in every street
Where comes the hurrying sound of human feet,
Are heard the cries of victory and defeat ;
The strife is never ending, day or night,
But weary warriors, resting from the fight,
May haply find, while sitting at a play,
Some word of cheer to help them on the way.

But the poor toiler, fallen at his task,
The stricken woman and the child, you ask,

How should the play help these? "The play's
 the thing
Wherein to catch the conscience of a king."
Why should not then its voice so far prevail
To win the generous ear, the heart assail,
Of such as yet may give some help to those
Who seek to ease the weight of human woes
And smooth the lot of toil, who would provide
A House where pain and anguish may abide,
Till rest and skill have made the wounded whole,
Or kindly death released the suffering soul?

 The world's a stage—a warfare—what you will,
Only let each his place, his part fulfil,
As we would ours to-night, with boon intent
To give a noble work encouragement,
The gift of rich men to the poor, or say,
Of those who thrive and prosper by the way
To those who fall, and without help would lie
In all the cruel crowd that hurries by,
Heedless though that one live, or this one die.

 And so the play may even be a mean
Of helping these, a kindly go between
From you to them, in their necessity,
Carrying the gathered boon you bring to see
The play, in pity's name. And why not so?
In pity's name, now ages long ago,
The fathers and the founders of the play

Did they not plead the cause I plead to-day?
Did they not teach the wealthy and the great
That they should help all those of low estate
Who fell, unfriended and unfortunate,
In the world's bitter war? And did not he,
The greatest of them all, for all who be
In dire extremes of pain and poverty,
Did he not make for such the mighty claim,
" That we should shake the superflux to them,
And show the heavens more just?" So in the play
Our wisest Shakespeare spake, so speaks to-day,
As if to you for sympathy appealing,
As if to those who build your House of Healing,
To all who give so nobly, at the call
Of those who work so nobly, and to all
Who have this gracious boon for toilers won,
It is as if his kind voice said, " well done!"

 Scorn not the play then, nor the players scorn,
They help the ideal, out of which is born
All that in all the world is worthiest,
Victoria Hospital among the rest.
Scorn not the play, the players, there may be
Much in them both with which we don't agree,
But so there is in everything we see.
In all things human good and evil grow
Together, but not therefore should we throw
Them both away together, false and true.

That's common, and 't is very easy too.
But not perhaps the wisest thing to do.

So, though some say that our good people are,
Oh, much too good to build a theatre,
Or when 't is built to call it by that name,
Though they do say it is one all the same,
Yet that shall not prevent nor you nor me
From reading Shakespeare, nor from going to see
The players on occasions, as select
As this, for instance, when we may expect
Performances that will be quite correct,
And where the comedy is free, I take it,
From all offence, unless you choose to make it.
But that I should not say, nor do I need
Before an audience like this to plead
Either for the play or the players; 't is most clear,
That these things, by your very presence here,
You heartily approve. And there is yet
Another matter we must not forget,
For which our gratitude is most sincere :
You all do know—strange as it may appear—
That even on occasions such as this
Our friends the amateurs have prejudice
To fight against. It may be, and indeed,
Is, no doubt honest, but narrow, and they need
Your help against the feeling we deplore :

And that they have.   And this—and this still
    more
Will reassure the simple and the sage—
You know the actors and their little stage
Are under " most distinguished patronage."

ESSAYS IN BLANK VERSE.

1848 1858

FAIRY FANCIES.

BENEATH a roof of immemorial trees
 That over-arch a pathway older still,
I walked along the sylvan aisles, moss-paven,
And while mine ear drank in the leafy hush,
Of whispering silence born, that seemed to fill
The trancèd spaces of the wood, I mused
That such a sweet and perfect solitude
Should hold no higher life, should be alone
The haunt of beast and bird, when 't were most fit
For rarest spirits a serene abode.
So much I mused of those traditions old,
Which, if ne'er true to the sense, unto the soul
Are true forever; that the woods were haunted
By woodland spirits who in grots and groves
Wove their free measures to the mystic pipings
Of old Silenus; for so it was reported
By those to whom they graciously revealed

Their hallowed haunts. But the quaint fauns
And satyrs dwelt not so remote as these,
For many a shepherd had been startled out
Of noontide slumbers in the tranquil woods
By their wild-echoing laughter, and at times
Had seen their grotesque visages out-peeping
From the rank underwood, and oft had heard,
Home wandering through the shadowy woods at
    night,
Feared by the loneness, the far distant sound
Of their immortal pipings, 'mazed, while they
Answered each other from their hidden bowers
In strains with which the eternal Pan himself
Had dared to challenge song's celestial sire.

And he, the shepherd-god, whose power
    encircled
The living universe, peculiarly
Delighted in the solemn woodlands, where,
Although unseen his mystic form divine,
His awful presence was revealed, what time
The mute winds slept on the broad leafy couch
Of mighty oaks vaulting the charmed air,
And conscious nature held her breath in awe;
When suddenly thorough the gloom profound
A wondrous whisper floated, wildering
The worshipping ear with sweet oracular tone :
Owned all things that mysterious utterance,

The windless forest waved spontaneous homage,
And the earth trembled at the voice of Pan !

Nor mused I mindless of time's later birth,
The elfin-forms our ancestors beheld
In every forest, every 'greenè shawe.'
To them the woodlands were not solitudes,
But fairy palaces where oft were seen
Fantastic revels 'neath the gleaming moon,
While spirit-echoes filled the archèd shade,
Faint as the lingering cadences that die
Among the wind-harp's strings.   But silent all
And disenchanted now the sylvan scene ;
The woodman plies all day his lonely task,
Day after day, night after night, comes home,
While moon and star-beams glimmer through
    the trees ;
No fairy tale brings he ; and men of the world
Being too enrounded with the throng of life,
And seldom walking in the antique woods,
Have long forgotten all their old-world lore.
Even those who fancy-charmed delight to roam
'Neath darkening branches, even these, although
Their eyes have fed upon the fair creations
Of dreamland, and their ears have been attuned
Unto the singing of the heavenly Muse,
Are blind unto those shapes of wonderment—

Are deaf to the remotest echoings
Of that strange minstrelsy—which in the thrall
Of their enchantments held the bodily sense
Of shepherds and of clowns whose simple lives
Were the beginnings of humanity!

Thus mused I in the solitary wood;
And though not all unmindful that the shapes
Once tenanting its dusky loneliness
Might be but shadows of a twilight world;
And, albeit, not forgetful that we now
Dwell in the presence of a purer light
By science shed over the dædal earth,
In whose divine effulgence are revealed
Beauty, and power, and marvel and delight
In natures erst obscure; and that the woods
In this calm light to the intellectual eye
Appear, indeed, temples divinely framed,
Most fitted by their natural solitude
To inspire high-pondering spirits with a sense
Of adoration's solemn ecstasies;
Yet from these thoughts my mind reverted still,
Heedless awhile of present influences,
And wrapt in half oblivious reverie,
Towards those dim enchantments of the past;
Partly because they seemed there to hold
Ancestral claim upon my reverence,

And partly for the love of loveliness,
Wherein these legends so transcend the world.

MOONRISE.

I WALKED beneath the calm, autumnal trees;
   I wandered through the mute, deserted
      woods :
I saw the sunset and the evening star
Come out above the tops of the dark pines
In the clear tranquil blue ; I lingered there,
Wrapt in the quiet beauty of the hour,
Watching the shifting lights and underglooms,
And listening to the sighing, sea-like sound
Of winter-boding winds. I waited still
Until the twilight deepened into dark
And the great moon had risen—the constant
      moon,
That ever watches with her patient smile
The nightly slumbers of her sister sphere.

There is one glory of the setting sun ;
There is another glory of the moon,
When far beyond the white cloud-canopy,

She lifts her lonely head among the stars,
And fills the earth with wonder, and the air
With wonder, and the underworld with peace.

INVOCATION.

THOU spirit of the living universe,
    Nature, mysterious name ! be thou to me
A comforter, as thou hast ever been,
Soothe me with thy all-gentle influences,
Uplift my soul above the thralls of time
Unto thy regions of eternal calm,
And I will be thy faithful acolyte,
My temple shall be thy blue canopy,
My altar there the earth-uplifted hills,
My robèd priest the ministering sun,
From flowery censers shall my incense rise,
The birds shall chant my matins, the free winds
Shall sing as listeth them my even-song,
And thou, the oracular intelligence
Of this thy starry universe, descend,
With intuitions from the infinite
Of God where thou abidest evermore,
With inspirations and sweet prophecies,

Visit thy worshipper, that so my feet
May fail not in thy service, that my heart,
Where sordid cares too oft have dwelt supreme,
May render at all seasons homage due
Of solemn reverence, and musèd praise,
And fancies high, and aspirations pure!

THE RIDGE OF SNOW.

MY Friend and I together o'er the ridge
    Of Pendle roamed; like hardy mountaineers
We scaled the steeps of snow; the winds of the
    north
Against our faces like a battle rushed,
With myriad edges keen, but up we pressed,
Trampling the snow beneath adventurous feet
And challenging the wind with laughter-shouts.
Ha, ha! 'twas rare, to breast the current strong
Of that aerial river, sweeping up
The snow in crystals of white, wintry splendour
Innumerable, until all the air
Shimmer'd with ice-beams, and 'twas rare to see
The weird devices which the frolic wind
Had wrought fantastic in the drifted snow:
Here a volute curled such as might have crowned
Ionian column; clustered there a wreath
Fit for Olympian victor; towered a crest
Achilles might have don'd to daunt old Troy;

And, lo, a cave with icy tapestries,
Which the fine needle of the frost had wrought
In such a web of wildering loveliness
As fairies weave to curtain dreams withal!
A cell of pearl, with crystal stalactites
And constellated gems! no nymph o' the sea
In the green waters ever found its like
Wherein to listen to the mystic song
Old ocean ever murmurs ; but a grot
Such as might Dian choose wherein to rest
Her white, smooth limbs and dream her pure,
    cold dreams
Beneath the waiting moon. And the moon waits,
But not for Dian—lonely is the hill
O'er which, as o'er a Titan's tomb, she seems
Her heaven-sad vigil keeping! For the night,
Her ancient nurse, she waits, her handmaid still,
Who thrones the sad queen mid her stars, till
    proud
Of her restorèd pomp she smiles. We, too,
Might there have lingered till the sun, declining
Over the sea, that seemed a path of light
Between the dim, blue mountains far away,
To happy islands of Elysian calm,
Had cleft the waters with his fiery wheels,
Stabling his steeds within those caverns cold,
That with the boom of ocean's myriad waves
Resound forever—and old Night had come

Out of her hall of shadows in the east ;
Had not tired limbs now warned us to return
To where the snug fireside would give repose
And leisure to talk o'er what we had seen,
And comfortably wonder how all looked
'Neath the cold gleam of starshine, when for each
Tremulous point and brilliant orb of gold
In the vast pomp and glory of heaven-dome,
A thousand gems would glisten on the hill
Of dazzling diamond and purest pearl,
And westward, lo, all silvery and serene,
The crescent moon crowning the silent scene !

Photo. Geo. Hy. Foulds.

OLD LODGE, TOWNELEY.

A WALK TO RED LEES
IN WINTER TIME.

SILENTLY in the silence of the night
    The thick snow fell; till all the quiet street
Was smooth and trackless as the farthest hill,
Whose whiteness glimmers in the white moon-
    shine.
Where'er it lay the wintry ground became
A pathway fit for feet angelical!
Whether around the porch with sculptured heads
Of saints adorned, beneath which worshipping
    throngs
With humble footsteps pass; or the dark mill
Where, with hoarse pants and mutterings harsh
    and deep,
Toils the blind Titan, Steam—the slave of wealth,
The tyrant of the millions who sweat
In fulsome rooms, while the sun shines without,
In summer on the broad, green woods and fields,
In winter on the snow; or whether it lies
Around the doors of shops, thence to be swept,

A thing that can be neither bought nor sold,
With little heed how beautiful it makes,
With its so peerless purity, the hard,
Black flags, where nothing half so fair,
So bright, through the long year hath ever lain :
Or down the stifling alley, close and foul,
Around the homes of crime and infamy,
Where its white stainlessness might win even
    hearts
Corrupted with the loathliest taint of sin
Back to the cleanest paths of virtue, save
That the deep curse of ignorance makes them
    blind !
O full of saddest pity 't is, to those
Who feel how near to some diviner world
Our human nature lies, the thought that here
The very impress of the tiny feet
Of children on the spotless ground should be
But the first track of footsteps that must go
Downward forever to still darker depths
Of hate and error, farther from the lights
Of divine knowledge—which is all divine—
That shine in the serene heights where mortal life
Touches the shores of immortality !
Yet here, amid the filthiest dens of vice,
The white snow with as blanched a smoothness
    lies
As where the violet sleeps beneath the sward.

Thither, ere breaks the dawn, let us away—
And as through yet untrodden streets we pass,
Where here and there lights gleam across the snow
From windows where the inmates are astir
Long ere the bell with iron clangour tolls
That calls them to their toil, we look, and, lo !
Those tasteless rows of dull formality,—
The dwellings of the poor—Oh, give them not
The rural name of cottage !—that have made
Our streets like barrack-buildings, where the throngs
Of labour eat and sleep between the hours
Of drill mechanical—and our dark towns
Unpicturesque and mean—even these square cells
Look beautiful, for over them the quaint,
Fantastic architecture of the snow
Has built its buttresses, its architraves,
Scrolls, columns, arches, gables, pent-house roofs,
And clusters like the tracery of flowers
Carved by the keen frost wind beneath the eaves.

And now we pass the church, around whose walls
The drifts are piled like marble bastions,
And to whose pinnacles the white flakes cling
Like delicate parasites.   The Catholic fane,

Named of the Virgin, where her image stands
Sandaled and crowned with snow !

                          To the old Lodge
With its grey towers we come. Ah ! many a year
Has passed away since in its rooms we slept,
To us so quaint and dim ; or lay awake,
Hushed to a wondering stillness by the roar
Of winds through the tall pine trees. Seldom now
We pass its gates, but we behold the shapes
Of those who have been dead so many years,
Walking in that old garden, passing in
And out of those old doors, in the old hall
Sitting between the great screen and the fire.
How sad and lonely is the house wherein
The dead remain ; where shadows walk from room
To room, with noiseless feet; where children play
Whose laughter is unheard ; where voices call
Through silent chambers on beloved names !
Now on its roof a battlement of snow
Rises o'er that of stone, dazzlingly pure.
Once in the room beneath, there lay the form
Of a young maiden, delicate and fair ;
In the old winters, when the snow lay thick
As it does now, on tower, and tree and shrub,
And round the mullioned window wreathed itself

In shapes fantastical, and the same moon
Silvered its pearly lustre, in the soft
And curtained twilight of that room she slept,
While not a sound disturbed her breathings calm ;
And there she died:—yet doth she lie there still,
Tranquil, and pure, and pale and beautiful
As she who slumbered for a hundred years
In the old legend which our childhood loved.

Along the stream, against whose bank the snows
Rise in sheer upright cliffs, and here and there
Beetle o'er caves of ice ; across the fields,
On whose smooth surface eddying winds have left
Tracks as of waves upon the ribb'd sea-sand,
Or sweeping curves, such as the midnight fays
Upon the gleaming, argent floor might leave,
As in wild dance their shadowy footsteps move,
In her high zenith while the moon shines cold !—
Beneath the trees that wear a fleecy robe
As lovely as the foliage of spring,
And up the hill we pass, until at length,
The summit gained, behold a prospect broad,
Of hill and dale, o'er which the golden dawn
Without a cloud is breaking. Wide above,
Its crescent gleams with tints ethereal,
Arched o'er a wider wilderness of snow !

LEGENDS OF PENDLE FOREST.

1848-1858.

" Thou hast discovered some enchantment old."
                                        —*Shelley.*

"Upon the eastern side of yon dark hill
Whose broad ridge frowns o'er Clitheroe's castled pride
And these monastic solitudes, the still
Abodes of ancient peace, lies lone and wide
A haunted region, wild and terrible,
Where spirits nor of earth nor heaven abide,
And, ruling o'er the dim, unhallowed air,
Enslave to fierce desires the dwellers there."
                                        —*Friar Dorien.*

MALKIN TOWER.

"Child Roland to the dark tower came."
— *Old Ballad.*

WHERE the drifting shadows rolled
    Over Pendle, drear and lone,
Midway on the barren wold,
Midway in the ages old,
    Stood a time-worn keep of stone.

Wild weeds grow and weeds of bane
    By the Forest's lonely way,
But of that dark Tower remain
Stead nor stone on steep or plain,
    But a memory void and vain,
    And a legend old and grey.

Wise in all forbidden lore,
    Master of the mystic wand,
Lord of many spells, who bore
Evil sway in Malkin hoar,
    Was the Wizard Hildebrand.

Dwarfish Hugo, treacherous loon
    Waited on his wicked will,
Waited not for hire or boon,
For an hour that cometh soon
    Is he watching, waiting still.

And the white maid Imobel,
    Daughter of the Wizard doure,
On her feet there is a spell,
In her chamber she doth dwell,
    Lonely, in the lonely Tower.

Shut within that Tower of bale,
    How should any know her doom?
How should any help avail?
How should Roland of the vale
    Know the hour when he must come?

Love is strong, and strong is hate,
  But the Wizard's evil power
Wise to know and slow to wait,
Cruel as relentless fate,
  Lords it in that evil hour.

Hovering o'er that Tower of stone,
  Night-birds bode with brooding wings,
Watching in her bower alone,
Till the gloaming grey is gone,
  Thus the hapless maiden sings :

> Mary Mother, maiden mild,
> Bring me to thy blessed Child,
> Pray, and say, and sing for me,
> Miserere, Domine !

> Mary Mother, Queen of Heaven,
> Sing for me thy angels seven,
> Pray, and say, and sing for me,
> Miserere, Domine !

Comes a footstep to the door—
  Is it Hugo, or her sire?
The Wizard ! bent with age and hoar,
With haggard eyes that evermore
  Roll, burning with a restless fire.

Thrice he waves his wand around,
    Thrice he weaves the mighty spell,
And, while in trancèd slumber bound,
He lifts her softly from the ground,
    And bears her to his secret cell.

Angels guard her tranquil sleep,
    Hovering on white wings! But mark—
Is it Hugo that does creep
So stealthily along, and peep
    Ever forward through the dark?

Noiselessly the Dwarf goes past,
    With his shambling feet all bare,
Now he glideth slow, now fast,
Now stands motionless, and last
    Crouches by the turret stair.

Now he turns, with treacherous hands
    Unbars the postern of the Tower;
In the dark a dark form stands,
And Roland of the vale demands
    "Are all things ready for the hour?

I dared thee once, I trust thee now ;
    As thou hast said so let it be."
The Dwarf replies, with sullen brow,
" The love of Imobel seek'st thou,
And I to hell have made a vow—
    It is enough—come follow me !

Thou knowest all,—it is the night
    His forfeit soul that he may save,
With many a dark and damned rite,
    He seeks to take the life he gave !
The hour of doom is come—the light
Is burning and the steel is bright.—"
    " Why then do we linger, slave !"

" Slow and sure—wouldst thou provoke
    All the fury of his spell,
The waving wand's avenging stroke,
The swift, keen curses that invoke
    To his aid the powers of hell !

Hadst thou felt—But listen now—
    If thou hold thy lady dear—
Neither Imobel nor thou
Ever leave this den, I trow,
    Once he waves that rod of fear !"

" I will dash it from his hand ! "
" Aye, or perish !—and then bear
Thy prize away."   " And Hildebrand ? "
" I fear no wizard without wand,
   Leave the dotard to my care."

" Harm him not ! "   " Ho, ho, not I,
   The devil will take him off my hand !
I'll have steeds the postern nigh
Matching hell for fleetness— Fly
   With the maiden where they stand."

Mary keep thee, Imobel,
   In this hour of fear and fate ;
Roland wight and Hugo fell
Now the turret stair do scale,
   One for love, and one for hate.

Another moment and they dare
   The Wizard in his den, and, lo,
In the midnight of her hair,
Imobel lies lifeless there,
   Still as marble, white as snow.

Captive to enchantments drear,
    Sinless in a dream of sin,
Powers of darkness hovering near,
All without, a nameless fear—
    Blessed Mary's peace within.

Horror-blinded Hildebrand,
    Muttering spell and weaving charm,
Watches pale the wasting sand,
Sees he not that daring hand
Raised to strike the wizard-wand
    From his weak and palsied arm?

No—'tis done—and Hugo dare
    Seize him now in grip of hate;
Roland down the gloomy stair
Does the spell-bound maiden bear
    Swiftly through the postern gate.

Champing fierce the fiery bit,
    Horses there stand ready dight;
Twin-born demons of the pit,
And their lamping eyes are lit
With fires o' the fen, that flare and flit
    About the moors at dead of night.

Swift he mounts the mighty steed,
    Foremost of the fiery twain,
For life, and love and loving heed,
Eager to prove his utmost speed
    And give him all the impatient rein.

Then towards the postern he,
    Curbing with unwilling hand,
Looks for Hugo—can it be
Him who comes so hastily?
    Heavenly powers—'tis Hildebrand!

How he 'scaped Dwarf Hugo's might,
    By what desperate charm and deep,
Roland, on that fearful night,
Heeds not, but with arrowy flight
    Plunges headlong down the steep!

Stormy is the night and dark,
    Darker still it gathers o'er him,
Black without a star, and hark,
How the fiend-winds howl and bark!
    Not his horse's head before him

Can he see, save for the flashes
  Of his brute and burning eyes,
Yet o'er moor and mere he dashes,
Where his feet the brown burn washes,
  Holding safe his holy prize.

For he hears the Wizard doure
  Chasing him on Hugo's steed,
Desperate to appease the infernal power,
O'ertake the midnight, murdering hour,
  And from impending doom be freed.

Fly the swift, pursuing fate !
  Urge amain that wondrous horse—
Heedless, if for one hour's date,
Holding still that lightning rate,
  Speeds he on his furious course.

How the weird winds storm and swell,
  And with fiend-like fury beat
On Roland and on Imobel,
Yet he shields her close and well,
  Wrapt in rest from head to feet.

Well for her the triple charm,
　　Dark-inwoven, dreamless, deep,
All unfearful she of harm,
All unfeeling of the storm
　　Buffeting her gentle sleep.

Well for him his daring soul,
　　For the night-hags far and near,
Imp, and ghoul and phantoms foul,
Troop and gibber, shriek and howl,
　　Exulting in the mad career.

Do not these his heart afear?
　　On his cheek that moment fell
A storm of rain-blown tresses dear;
And his heart beats high and clear,
　　Unappalled by ugliest hell.

So the doom-driven desperate twain
　　Through the dreary Forest go,
Not a rood does either gain,
Though the first the first remain,
Close behind him echoes plain
　　The hoof-thunder of his foe.

MALKIN TOWER.

Whither, whither do they speed?
  Roland neither knows nor cares.
If a while his mighty steed
Keep him of the fiend ahead,
  Through the darkness on he dares.

Like a storm o'er flood and fell,
  Headlong as the bolt of heaven,
On they drive, as though one will
Of fiend or fury urged them still,
  To one doom of darkness driven.

Hoof to hoof!—But can it be?
  In his perilous career
Roland's steed sinks prone—and he
Forward thrown upon his knee,
  Holds the tranced maiden there.

Desperate then, with sudden bound,
  He turns to face the coming doom.
Fiercely turns—but wide around
All is still, and not a sound
  Comes across the pathless gloom!

Round he stares, with breathless heed—
Whither sped the Wizard drear!
Where the steed, whose fiery speed
Failed him at his utmost need?
  All the phantoms, all the fear,

Vanish like dreams into the night—
  And the dark and triple charm
Passes from the maiden bright,
As the doom-driven Wizard wight
  Passes with the passing storm.

And with wide and wondering eyes
  Imobel, so still and fair,
Sees the midnight moon arise,
Sees a dream of starry skies,
  And a new enchantment there.

"Roland!" "Imobel!" And, lo,
  How trustingly the white arms cling:
Now, plighting hand in hand, they go
By woodland ways they seem to know,
Where steep crags o'er the pathway throw
  The shadow of an eagle's wing!

And through the narrow pass they roam,
    Far down the deep, romantic dale;
Where, in a wild, sequestered home,
The maiden's cheek again will bloom,
And parting sorrow never come
    To her or Roland of the Vale!

Who is Lord of Malkin now,
    Where the lonely Tower doth stand?
Never more that Tower of woe
Lord or habitant did know,
    Since the doom of Hildebrand.

Lord or habitant, save whom
    'Tis not meet that I should name,
For, when nights with tempest loom,
From that lonely turret-room
    Flashes far a ghastly flame.

And amidst the wild alarm,
    When lightnings fall with many a jag,
A spectral horseman's shadowy form
Driveth with the driving storm,
    From Malkin Tower to Eagle's Crag!

So sung the legendary rhyme,
  A bard who loved the moorland vale,
The haunted bourne, the barren clime,
The shadows of that hill sublime,
  The Forest, where he found the tale.

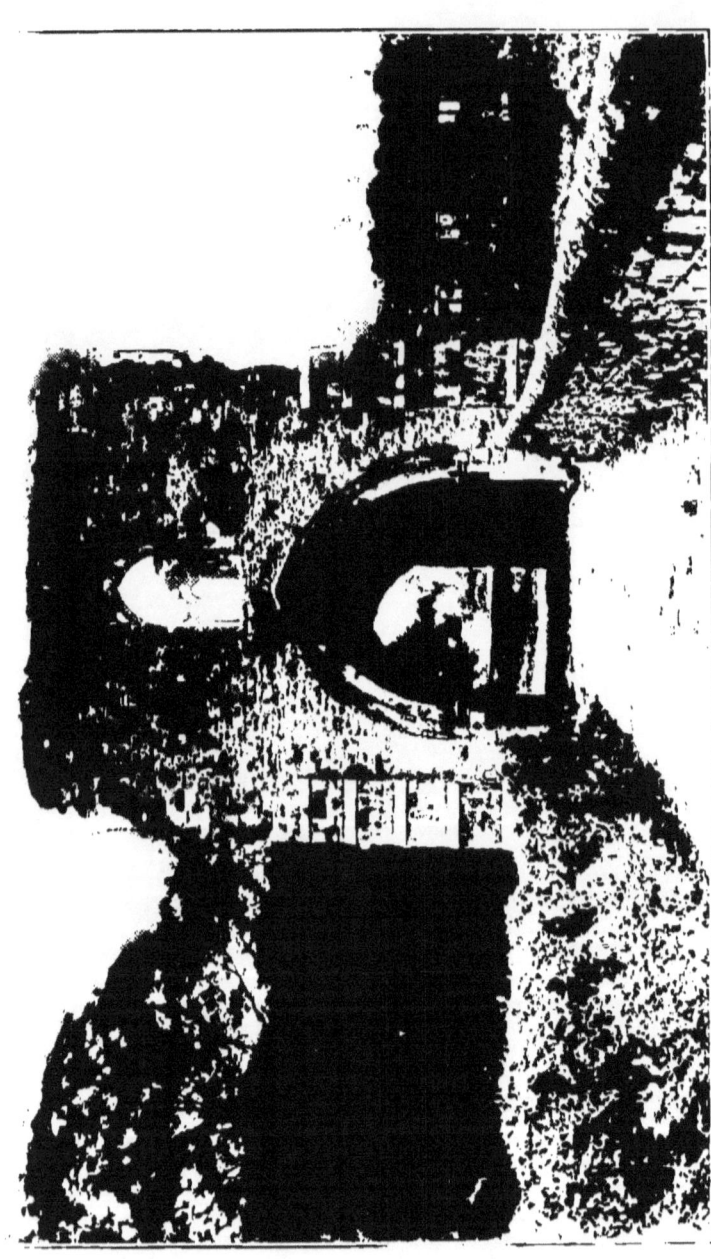

Photograph by] ENTRANCE GATEWAY, WHALLEY ABBEY. [F. Frith & Co., Reigate.

FRIAR DORIEN.

> "Where have you been, sister?"
> "Sister, where you?"
> —*Macbeth.*

FRIAR Dorien, a holy man was he;
    Of all the monks of Whalley there were few
Whom the old Abbot loved so brotherly;
For ever walked he in obedience due
To saintly discipline, and still would be
Foremost in all good offices, a true
Servant of Christ, in word, and thought, and deed,
And never missed an ave or a creed.

To early matins cheerfully he hied,
And oft would linger in the twilight dim,
After the last, low cadences had died
Up the long aisles of the sweet vesper hymn;
The services of every holy-tide
Full well he knew, and much it soothèd him
To join the choral chant when prayers were said,
And solemn masses offered for the dead.

In the calm, blissful sunset—long ago,
With him the good old Abbot many times
Measured the mossy pathway to and fro
Of the o'er-arching avenue of limes,
Between the Calder, gliding smooth and slow,
And the dark porch o'er which the ivy climbs;
And ere the western clouds grew dun and pale
On the grey sky, the monk had told his tale.

"Good Father! 'tis not well that we should call
Back to the mind its memories of pain,
Save when before thee in confessional
We kneel for absolution from the stain
Of fore-committed sin; and yet withal,
I at thy bidding will live o'er again
A dreary time; albeit, I may seem
As one who talketh of some hideous dream.

"Upon the eastern side of yon dark hill,
Whose broad ridge frowns o'er Clitheroe's castled
    pride,
And these monastic solitudes—the still
Abodes of ancient peace—lies lone and wide,
A haunted region, wild and terrible,
Where spirits nor of earth nor heaven abide,
And, ruling o'er the dim, unhallowed air,
Enslave to fierce desires the dwellers there.

"A savage land! From yonder hill it takes
The name of Pendle Forest—known afar
For the dark deeds of fierce demoniacs,
Who, leagued with Sathanas, wage evil war
On all whom innocence or virtue makes
Fit objects of their hate: no baleful star,
No charmed essence, no malignant hour,
But these dread beings can command its power."

"Full well I know," the Father Abbot said,
"That land of fear, that realm of sorcery!
And surely that steep mountain rears its head
To shelter these abodes of piety
From powers unblest." And here in holy dread
He crossed himself and told his rosary,
And the good Dorien crossed himself as well,
And thus in gentle tones resumed his tale.

"The joys of youth—ah benedicite!
How frail, how vain, how swiftly they are gone,
And yet how they endure in memory!
So shall I ne'er forget the sylvan Brun
Where as a child I played, a boy with free
And fearless footsteps roamed from sun to sun,
Where wandering in youth I found a dream
  That threw enchantment round that lonely
    stream.

"'Twas love. O Father! I to thee have told
In sad confession all my errors past;
What boots it, then, that I again unfold,
How, driven by adverse fate, I sought the last
Refuge of hope among those warriors bold,
Who on the fields of France made death aghast
With slaughter; whence with booty I returned,
While eager hope within my bosom burned.

"I rode through rich domains of wood and wold,
Yet still before me rose the cottage dear
Where Anabel dwelt with her mother old;
Until at length, far in the distance clear,
The sable bulk of Pendle I behold,
And urge my steed, for night is gathering near;
Impatient love the nearest path will dare,
So towards that haunted Forest on I fare.

"But as I passed beneath the steep ascent,
Darkness o'er all the dreary prospect fell:
Not such a night as now from heaven is sent
Upon these solitudes monastical,
Slow, tranquil, soothing, and beneficent;
But sudden, dense and supernatural,
O'er all the gloomy air with black mists blent,
While howling winds to howling winds did moan
Through all that region desolate and lone!

"Yet on through that enchanted Forest wide
I took my fearless course, with little care
How spectral shadows might around me glide,
My starting steed how impish horrors scare,
Upon the phantom-winds though witches ride
With hootings dire far up the starless air,
My eager love not even these appal,
Nor the black mists built round me like a wall.

"Mile after mile, through dangerous paths obscure,
And darkness still o'er all the charmèd ground !
Till, of my further course at length unsure,
I curbed my weary steed and gazed around;
Just then, a lurid ray of light impure
Streamed fitfully athwart the gloom profound,
And with impatient spur my steed I turned
Towards where that red beacon fiercely burned.

"Ere long unto a dark and lonely Tower
I came, of aspect horrible and grim,
As though the spell of some malignant power
Had built with curses every turret dim !
All black and silent as the midnight hour,
Save for the topmost loophole's ghostly gleam,—
Till suddenly, from wall, and roof and rafter,
There burst shrill sounds of wild, unearthly laughter.

"I had an amulet of mickle might,
Of wondrous virtues it was wrought, I ween;
'Twas given to me by a dying knight
Whose comrade in the war I erst had been;
He said its power from every evil sprite
Would still defend me. When that hideous din
Had sunk again to silence, with one hand
I grasped this charm, the other my good brand,

"And sought the entrance of that gloomy den,
A portal like a cavern's yawning mouth :
Within, a monstrous hound, with frightful mane
And flaming eyes and ghastly jaws uncouth,
Stood glaring! Horror held my footsteps then,
But oh! The wondrous amulet was sooth;
The fiend shrunk from it with a baffled howl
Into the darkness, where I heard him growl.

"Anon, I found the turret's winding stair,
And, groping up, at every turn I came
Upon some sudden horror unaware!
A hooded shadow, lit with eyes of flame;
A weeping corpse, with murder in its hair;
A phantom face, that never seemed the same;
A gorgon blind, with serpents in its eyes;
And nightmares huge, and impish atomies!

"But oh! the wondrous, potent amulet—
These forms infernal vanished as I clomb.
But no phantasmal shapes were those that set
Mine eyes astare i' the wind-rocked turret room,
But the weird sisters of the Forest, met
To frame their dark conspiracies of doom,
Their deeds of impious revenge to tell,
On all who might provoke those hags of hell.

"And thus it chanced I came upon them then
In exultation fierce. 'Ha, ha!' cried one,
'From Raven's Nest, i' the Vale of Todmorden,
Hither away beneath a misty moon,
I took the crow's flight over moor and fen;
And I bring ye news, rare news;—the miller's son
Whom I frighted a' nights with a haunting horrible sound,
Deep in the pool beside the mill lies drowned.'

"Another came from Eagle's Crag, she said,
Where she had sat in semblance of an owl,
Blinking and hooting her enchantments dread,
And filling the thick air with poisons foul,
That rack with torture every nervy thread,
And fill with fever-phantasies the soul,
Till she saw pass through the dismal dell below,
Breathing that venom-dew,—her mortal foe.

"And then a ghastly shape, withered and blear,
Leapt like a palsy from behind the flame!
With dotard accents and malignant leer,
Screaming—' Ha, beldames! wist ye whence I
    came?
'Tis not for nought that ye behold me here;
Ye knew the cottage, and ye knew the dame,
And eke the winsome Anabel, I trow,—
That lonesome cottage will be lonelier now!

"'Yon dull imp Madge in my despite would pray
Before the cross that stands in Brunshaw Lane,
And when I pinched and pined her all the day,
Stole off at night to yonder meddling twain
Who dared to rate me for a witch, and say
I was a cruel stepdame thus to train
The innocent child;—ha, ha! they little knew
Whose vengeance on their heads they rashly
    drew.

"'For standing there, I cursed them in my hate,
Not with vain words, but with as dire a spell
As e'er was woven in the loom of fate,
That wrought even as the banning accents fell,
The mother died while the night-ravens sat
Croaking upon the roof, and Anabel
Did slowly craze and dwindle, peak and pine,
And died, ere hours were numbered nine times
    nine.

"'Is't not a dainty tale ? If ye want proof,
Up, sisters, on the wing and follow me !'
Again yelled out the laughter, while aloof
I stood as in a trance of agony,
While all that cursed crew through the rent roof
Did vanish, shrieking their infernal glee ;
And still I stood there trembling in the cold,
For well I knew of whom the tale was told.

"O Father Abbot ! urge me not to tell
The desolation of that fearful morn,
When all too true I found that dream of hell,
And standing in the ruined hut forlorn
Vowed to devote in some monastic cell
My life and wealth to heaven, that those I mourn
I may remember still when prayers are said,
And solemn masses offered for the dead."

"'Thy tale," the Abbot said, "is strange, my son,
And yet, I trow, 'tis not more strange than true,
For in that dark, enchanted Tower 'tis known,
Those hags of mischief many a witch-charm brew,
With which they scatter misery and moan ;—
The saints defend us from the unholy crew !"
And as they passed the ivied gateway, old,
The solemn convent bell for Vespers tolled.

THE WHITE WITCH.

"Beauty and anguish walking hand in hand,
The downward slope to death."
— *Tennyson.*

I.

A TALE of the times of old—when Pendle Hill
Looked o'er a lonely region, wild and bare,
Where the white smoke of hamlet or of farm
Was seldom seen amid the silent waste
Of bosky mere, brown moor or marish green :
Far in the north the hills of Westmorland
Rise like Hadean alps, and in the west
A low coast stretches, where the desolate sea
That washes Mona and the Cumbrian shores
Dashes its wild, unharboured waves in foam :
A land of many streams whose fountains rise
Where morning rises on the moors, and flow
Towards the sunset, down the rocky glens

And through the hollow valleys, tenantless,
Save by the wild fox that hath made its den
Beneath the cliffs, or where the lonely hern,
Watched by the hawk, is watching in the pool,
With rushes fringed and tall green water-flags :
Of old the eternal stars had mirrored there
Their pure, essential fires. Midway between
These sheltered vales remote and that bleak hill,
Upon the sylvan slopes of one of these
Wild mountain burns, a lonely mansion reared
Its gabled roof among o'er-shadowing woods
Of pine, and sycamore and yew trees old,
Beneath whose branches the swart, twilight elves
Unseen might hold their state. A lonely place,
Where dwelt a lonely lady, beautiful,
Reserved and stately as a crownèd queen :
The Sorceress, Magdalen! Her proud, fair face
The golden prime of early womanhood
Had scarcely sobered, ere in fatal hour
And fiery stress of passion she had bent
Rebellious to the dark rebellious powers,
Offering her heritage of heavenly bliss
That they for some brief while to her might yield
Obedience, doing her imperious will.
The years of her proud sway were numbered, yet,
Ere half their course, Azrael had numbered her's,
And she must die.

This lady had a child,
Sole offspring of a most unhappy time,
That should have been most happy, loved, as she
Alone could love whose heart was now a void,
Deep, silent, like a hollow alpine gulf
Whose craggy darkness one sole star illumes!
A child in years, in innocence, with all
Her mother's pride of feature and of form,
But softened into beauty like the moon,
With all her still severity of soul,
Equal to mighty darings, and yet pure
As the white snows of Atlas that upbear
The destinies of heaven. A glorious child!
Walking through time's dark labyrinths of fear
With angel instincts—such was Agatha.

Within a wide and tranquil chamber, lit
With taper dim that hideth not the light
Of moonbeams falling through the diamond
    panes
Of the deep oriel on the oaken floor,
Kneels Agatha beside the dying Witch—
Her mother, beautiful and so beloved!
A silver Crucifix whereon was graven
The incarnate Lord of everlasting Love,
Hung round her white neck by a crimson band,
Silken, with clasps of gold. This she uplifts
In her pure hands and prays, and as she prays,

Her voice so sweet, her seraph-pleading tones
Throb with the broken music of despair.
For, ah! her mother prays not; cannot pray.
Some Evil Power broods o'er her like a cloud,
Shutting out heaven : and there she lies aghast,
With fixèd gaze and panting sobs of pain.
Some vague and threatening horror! Agatha,
Becoming conscious of that Presence dark,
Looks up towards it, then with sudden cry,
She buries her blanch'd face upon the bed,
While the strong tremor of her grief shakes loose
Her gleaming hair, whose mass of clustering gold
Shieldeth her innocent head from that dim Fear;
And in low voice where love and misery blend
Their tones together in strange unison,
She mourneth, "Mother, mother, mother mine,
Is there no power in heaven to avert
The destinies of hell? Has Christ, who gave
His heart to the sharp spear of agony,
Not so much love as one weak heart can hold,
Who would give all her everlasting hopes
For thy lost soul?" Thus 'plains she in her woe.
Impatient of her anguish, she would dare
To break its spell, the darkest doom of all.
Unweeting she, poor child, how terrible
The ordeal she has challenged. Well for her,
That on her gentle heart such trial fierce
Will never be imposed. But say not so!

For while she lieth prone in her despair,
She feels that mystic Presence darkening
Above her head, while shadowy whispers strange
Come to her ear alone. "Give soul for soul—
Thy soul for her's—and I will take the spell
From off her tongue—the curse from off her
    heart.
Make her bond thine! Take off the Cross thou
    wearest
And swear no mortal hand shall e'er restore it—
And that shall be the sign." Motionless there
Lies Agatha, as though that dreadful voice
Had frighted from her heart the pulse of life.
A dreary time she lies; and in that room
Dead silence reigns, as though the powers of air
Were waiting her resolve. At length she hears
Her mother's faint, quick breaths begin to fail,
And in that moment of intensest hush
She rises slowly, calmly, deadly pale;
And with her cold, fair fingers steadily
She takes that crimson thread from her white
    neck,
And, bending o'er her mother tenderly,
In silence vows the vow, and lays the Cross
Upon her dying bosom.
                           'Tis enough!
With a faint smile of peace upon her face,
A prayer upon her lips and in her heart,
Departed then the soul of Magdalen!

II.

Who now is so forlorn as Agatha,
In that dark house, day after day alone ;
From morning, when the cold and scornful light
Laughs in the weak, wan eyes of misery,
Till evening like a slow, stern jailor comes
And shuts her in with darkness and despair.
Night after night alone, while fiend-driven winds
Howl thro' the desolate pines, in mockery
Of all her mute, unutterable woe ;
Or while they sleep, star-charm'd, on the broad slopes
Of legend-haunted Pendle, undisturbed,
Save by some lonely night-bird's maniac-scream ;
And o'er the house, whose walls are echoless
As charnel vaults, the nightmare, silence, broods,
Whose spell lies heavy on her beating heart,
And her hushed breathings, regular and slow.
No faintest whisper that dead stillness breaks,
No soft tones vibrate through the listening air,
No gentle voices through the tranquil rooms
Shall ever call the name of Agatha ;
Never in book, or song or legend old,
Did any read, or hear or dream of one

So young, so beautiful, so lost as she!
Tears 'have been shed ere now in the olden
    time,'
But not on her their comforting dews may fall,
Or soothe her unparticipated grief.
No earthly sympathy, no heavenly hope
Are hers; alone, and utterly forlorn
She must remain in her deserted home:
Yet not alone; ah, would it were but so—
For, O ye pitying saints of heaven! and thou
Compassionate Maid! to whom 'all woful cry,'
Tho' ye have all forsaken her, tho' shunned
By men and angels, she is not alone.
She bears the burden of her mother's sin,
Her mother's punishment, forevermore:
The burden of a Presence that makes dark
The golden day, and thickens night with fear.
That Evil Power broods o'er her like a cloud,
Shutting out heaven:—the dark Familiar—
The ever-present, ministering Fiend—
Slave of the bond—or angel of the doom
That from her mother's soul she freely took
And laid upon her own. Poor Agatha!
What should she do with the forbidden powers
Of sorcery—the agencies of hell,
Who never hated any living thing,
Nor had a wish save one—to be beloved.
Yet still it haunts her—shadowy now and dim

It seems before her—now behind her moves
An unseen Terror—sometimes in the gloom
Of evening, as she paces restlessly
The darkening rooms, two fiery eyes will burn
Fiercely through hers; or sitting weary down,
With vacant eye fixed on the vacant air,
That ghastly Incubus is crouching too,
And from the clinging horror come again
Those shadowy whispers strange: she feels, not
    hears,
The supernatural tones that fascinate
As with a weird, unearthly melody.

"Once among the sons of morning
    Seraph-born Azazil stood;
In his haughty spirit scorning
    All who scorned his servitude;
Who preferred to heavenly bliss
Freedom in the vast abyss.

Who on wide and daring pinions,
    Through infinitudes of thought,
Through the unexplored dominions
    Of eternal darkness, sought
Fate's high secrets—which to find
Yearneth still the immortal mind:

All who dared transcend the vision
  Of the narrow realms of light ;
Dared to pass from homes Elysian,
  To the yawning gulfs of night,
Where the infinite profound
Looms above, beneath, around :

These the spirits of perdition,
  Deemed Azazil in his pride,—
The dark angels whom ambition
  In rebellious league allied ;
Till to outer darkness driven,
Exiled from the thrones of heaven.

But, though all the mysteries hidden
  In the fathomless obscure,
Could not move to thoughts forbidden
  That proud Seraph's soul secure,
Love could tempt him to resign
Heaven for pleasures more divine.

For among the angelic powers
  Whom the light of mortal eyes
Drew from the ethereal towers
  Of their vaunted paradise,
With the maids of earth to dwell,—
Seraph-born Azazil fell !

Fell—but not to fabled regions,
  Where, in fires Hadean chained,
Expiate the rebel legions
  The ambition that disdained
Heaven —the heaven he left unmourned,
Descending to the abyss he scorned.

Since, through starry glooms he fareth,
  On, from world to world, he flies,
And wherever beauty weareth
  Sorrow in her radiant eyes,
Woos her soul to pleasures high,
To delights that never die.

He full many a spell divineth
  Sullen minds from grief to lure—
If for love the maiden pineth,
  Haunted with ideals pure,
She shall learn its words of fire
From lips of passionate desire.

If dark dreams of melancholy,
  Or of supernatural fear,
Bind her soul with spells unholy,
  To Azazil let her ear,
Her thoughts, her heart, surrendered be,
And from that moment she is free :

Fables old of Hell and Heaven
   Shall perplex her faith no more ;
Unto her it shall be given
   With the immortals to explore
Mysteries of essential being,
Known unto the gods all-seeing.

If her soul, intensely yearning,
   Claim Seraphic sympathies,
Where the farthest stars are burning
   In the deep abysmal skies,
She shall roam on wings of light
Through nameless Edens of delight.

The sweet dreams that mortals never
   Realize of human love,
Or of joys that reign for ever,
   Crowned and garlanded above,
Show like shadows, faint and dim,
To her beloved of Seraphim !

Who would brood o'er earthly sorrow,
   Who to earthly love would bend,
Who of hope would comfort borrow,
   When in accents that descend
On the heart like balmy dews
Seraph-born Azazil woos!

The dark voice ceased, like a rich tune that dies
Upon the ear of sorrow unconsoled:
Bewildered was the soul of Agatha.
Her poor thoughts wandered through its sophistries
Like thirsty bees that haunt the poison-flowers
They dare not taste. Sometimes the sweet, sad tones
With tears of a strange sympathy would fill
Her weary eyelids; then a white, cold fear
Would creep around her heart, as thought recurr'd
To that dark Presence, to the death-bed dark
It made so ghastly; till upon her mind,
Perplexed with conflict of emotions wild,
Almost to madness, that sweet smile of peace
Which on her mother's dying face had shone,
With most ineffable meanings, came again,
Came like an inspiration, as the voice
Ceased, and with silence a repose so deep
And sudden o'er her spirit soft descends,
That sinking back upon her cushioned seat
She slept with breathings calm.

     Rest, Agatha,
Devoted child of a strange destiny!
And may the slumbers o'er thy spirit stealing,
As white death beautiful, as death serene
And dreamless be. Sleep on, thou poor forlorn:

For, lo, upon thy patient features mild
The same sweet smile of peace thy mother wore
Of most ineffable meanings—when she died!

III.

O, for the wizard wand of Archimage,
Potent o'er airy messengers, to send
A sprite down deep to Morpheus, where he lies
In drowsy glooms of his Hadean hall,
Wrapt in eternal silence, for a draught
Of Lethe's soothing waters, or the fumes
Of deep-hued poppies that enrich the mists
Of that Tartarean stream with odours bland,
To deepen and prolong the slumbers kind
That lull the senses of lost Agatha!
But from this short oblivion she will wake
To years of mute and patient agony,
And, side by side with her self-chosen doom,
Shall measure her predestined course to the end
So swift and terrible. And yet through all,
And under all the weight of mortal fear,
Shall grow in beauty up to womanhood;
Shall seek, even in her utter hopelessness,
To live in deeds of charity; to bend
Even the powers of darkness to her aims,
Beneficent and pure.

In those dark times,
When evil powers were rife through all the land,
Was Pendle Forest famed, even as of old
Dodona's ancient wood, as the chief haunt
Of supernatural influence; for there
The fellest brood of fear that ever wrought,
By means infernal, deeds of cruelty
Were numerous as the birds of night, with whom
They made their haunts, and took strange flights
    afar,
Through the dim air, to ghastly rites obscene.
These many a deed of hate had wrought around
Agatha's lonely home, till she was moved
By sore constraint of pity to compel
That dread Familiar,—waiting still to yield
His evil service—grudgingly to obey
Her pure behests of love;—those hags of hell
To baffle, and their deeds of sin subvert,
By agencies as potent as their own.
Thus many innocent and helpless souls
Were rescued from malicious cruelty,
And fierce inflictions dire and terrors wild.

And now the fame of Agatha, her life
Of loneliness in that deserted house,
Her most immaculate beauty—wherein some
Beheld a higher grace than mortal mould

Might wear, unclothed with heavenly sanctity—
Her nameless doom of sorrow, and that power,
Strange, yet beneficent, at which who most
Blessed it did wonder most—spread far and wide;
And all who felt the power of spells malign,
Racking the frame with anguish, wasting slow
The life-blood drop by drop, or all the soul
Darkening with weird enchantments horrible,
Sought the White Witch, for such the name she
    bore
In hut and hall, where'er her power was known,
And she restored them to the peaceful flow
Of happy breath, and pulse unthrobbed with
    pain.
At length, defeated, baffled, desperate,
Those hags of spite conspired a deadly charm,
More swiftly, terribly inevitable,
Than ever Hecat brewed in the midnight air
To fright the world with pestilence and death.

    But leave we those dark beings to their foul
Conspiracies of hate, and turn again
To the doomed maid forlorn. In that old house,
Loneliest of all the lonely rooms, was one
Haunted with shadows of a happier time,
Wherein there stood an antique cabinet,
Whereon were carved wing'd angels with clasped
    hands

And supplicating eyes, and underneath
Grim, monstrous heads, grinning with features
    wild
Of fiendish phantasy; above were placed
Caskets and silver vessels, objects rare
Of quaint device,—priceless with memories old;
And over all the silver Crucifix
Which, with its crimson band and clasps of gold,
Had hung there since the death of Magdalen.
'Twas like an altar-place, where solemn prayers
Are offered up, and fuming censers waved
With spiced incense burning. Here would come
That solitary maid, and kneel before
The God whose love her love had forfeited
For long sad hours,—yet not her saddest hours;
For though she could not pray, though not a word
Her lips could frame to ease her yearning heart,
Yet she would kneel, and gaze and feel the peace
Of calm and heavenly influences descend
From that cross-tortured form, those angels mild,
And from the shadowy shapes of human love
That haunted there, on her so desolate heart.

Oh, had I gold to buy some painter's skill
To paint me Agatha, kneeling there alone,
With beautiful eyes serene and forehead pure,
Crowned with her bright, seraphic hair, and mute

Enchanted lips that seemed to wait the touch
Of angel fingers opening them to prayer!

One eve she came not at the accustomed time,
And o'er the cabinet the Crucifix
Gleams not as heretofore.   Where is it gone?
And where is Agatha?   It is the night
When that dark charm is wrought which all the land
Shall desolate with a swift, nameless curse;—
And she is gone to brave those witches dark
In their own haunts, and baffle all their spite
By one last resource. Through the homeless ways
Of darkness, through the dreary haunted glens
Of Pendle Forest, she is roaming on—
Through stormy winds, heavy with midnight mists
That drench her tangled hair and silken stole,
And her wan cheeks and lips that coldly kiss
The falling tress, all comfortless and chill,
Driven by the gusty storm. For weary miles—
For weary, weary miles, she wanders on,
In silence and in solitude, through bleak
Untrodden paths, and wild forsaken wastes,
Encompassed with unknown and shadowy fears,
Yet all serene within, with eye serene,
The Pilgrim of Compassion passes on—
A sacrifice if need be to the rage
Of those revengeful. Hark, upon the wind!

She hears a rush as if of rustling wings :
The hags are hastening to their rendezvous ;
Though wingless they, yet swift and far their
    flight.
And hark again, mid yells and hootings dire,
She hears a cry, "Wilt ride, White Witch, wilt
    ride !
Up here, up here, or thou wilt be belated !"
And on they pass, and on she passes too,
Undaunted, and with high resolved will ;
She too hath power o'er airy ministers,
And to despise that power, for holier means
To-night are hers, which she will trust alone.
So through the moonless mist she journeys on,
Till to the desecrated steep she comes
Of Pendle, hoary hill of evil fame,
And as she climbs, with eager step, and breath
Panting, and eye of preternatural fire,
She hears the witch-chant intermittently
Borne on the wind, and hastens up, her heart
With big throbs pulsing. Now she gains the top—
And lo, a lurid flame, round which there dance
Gaunt forms, with eyes demoniac, and fierce
    grins,
With frenzied chattering, idiot gestures foul,
Whinings insane, impish, blood-chilling leers,
Horrible rampings, nightmare ghastliness !
And all the gorgon terrors bedlam sin

Can borrow from the fiends. These round the
    flames,
Illumining fitfully their contortions wild,
Dance dismally, howling this chorus bleak :—

On the top of Pendle old,
Pendle Hill, so dark and cold,
Round about the bale-fire sing,
In the seething cauldron fling,
Mixt in magical proportions,
Reptile poisons, imp abortions ;
All the bitter weeds of death
Gathered on the blasted heath,
When the moon is in her cave,
Or beneath the heaviest wave
Of the deadly, wreck-strewn deep
Where the slimy monsters creep ;
Mineral essences malign
Gnome-distilled i'the pestilent mine ;
Noxious exhalations foul
Which the midnight-wandering ghoul
From the reeking tomb doth bring,
While the corpse is festering ;
Curses ending with the breath
On the grinning field of death ;
Maniac moan and murder yell ;—
Relics only fit for hell,

Relics rare of crime and sin,
Throw the reeking cauldron in:
And a meteor downward hurled
From a red and burning world,
Finishes the deadly spell;
Who a mightier charm can tell?
Till a mightier charm be found
Dance again the mystic round!

The incantation ceased; and now amidst
That horrid brood of sin stands Agatha,
With shining hair back-streaming luridly,
And countenance as fiercely beautiful
As the doom-angel's whose shrill voice of wrath
Shall tremble the firm stars. "Behold," she cried,
And held aloft the silver Crucifix!
All shrunk appalled, though some had menace dared,
Watching with hate and fear, as still she cried
"O, ye benighted, abject race and scorned!
Behold a mightier than your mightiest charms,
Though brewed in the deep pit of Acheron!
Thus do I prove its power!" and suddenly
She plunged it in the Stygian element.—

At once, fire, cauldron, witch-charm, all
Vanished with hissing fumes; and that grim crew,

Confounded, vanquished, panic-stricken, fled—
Fled through the impure air with hideous screams,
And o'er the dark hill night resumed her sway.

IV.

How calm—how cold—how beautiful—is death!
To those who dwell upon its tranquil rest—
Its deep, deep rest, perfect and full of peace:
A peace so far beyond what life affords
In stillest solitudes, or slumbers holy,
That, longing to forsake the world and all
Its tiresome, turbulent insanities,
Its restless dreams of care, we fain would seek
In death's cold shadow peace, and only peace.

To her of whom is told this tale of teen,
Death had not this fair aspect, had not this
Immortal atmosphere of grand repose;
But like a brooding terror threatened still
With darker fears her dark and fearful life.
Her life was like a dream whose haunting shapes
Are but the shadows of an unknown woe,
That even now shall wake the sleeper up
To some intenser horror. Even now—
For the dark hour approaches when the soul
Of Magdalen was forfeit to the bond
Whose burden Agatha must bear alone:

And she prepares to meet the coming doom
Inevitable, with rigid soul severe
Of patient, uncomplaining hopelessness.
To whom should she complain, uplifted thus
In high, immortal sorrow far above
The reach of mortal sympathy? To whom?
Earth could not credit her great grief; and heaven
Its golden ladder has updrawn, and now
Celestial influences no more descend,
No more ascend like angels plumed with prayer.
And can it be that one so white, so pure,
So full of every high and heavenly grace,
Shall be cast off for ever without aid
From all the thousand watchers of the skies?
Will heaven remain serene and undisturbed—
Will not a wing be ruffled, not a foot,
Sandalled with fire, be lifted?—By one way,
And only one, do mortal spirits fallen
Enter the heavenly homes, and that one way
She closed forever when the Crucifix
She took from off her breast and vowed the vow
That human hand should ne'er replace it there.
She knew the forfeit then, the doom she knew,
Accepted willingly without reserve,
So without hope she bears it evermore.
She would not any portion of the price
Should be unpaid which her heroic heart

Grudged not to offer for her mother's soul,
Lest, from secure abodes of peace down-hurled
To self-imposed destiny, be driven
The twice redeemed! No, let the dark hour come
Whose fixed fate her sleepless heart abides.

O Time! remorseless slave of Destiny,
Not fleeter o'er the hill the shadows fly
Of wind-swift clouds, than by thee driven the hours
Through day and night, in quick, alternate change,
Pass o'er that house of doom where Agatha
Waits with a wasting pulse and waning eye.

Without, the winds in inarticulate tones
Utter a weird, unearthly prophecy
To all the groaning pines, that in the light
Of the dim evening nod their sombre heads,
Like dark-robed priests, to some primeval fear
Offering strange rites insane. And, see, the moon
Has risen broad and dim behind the trees:
Ere it attain its zenith, in that dark
And lonely pile the doom will be complete,
That shall give all its mute, unhallowed walls
To bats, and owls and ruining winds, until

From gabled roof to deep foundation stone,
No vestige shall remain to tell a tale
Of haunting terrors to the after times.

Who is that sitting in the room alone?
Still dwells the soul within that wasted form?
In that thin, shadowy shape still beats the heart
Compassionate and pure? Breathes that worn frame,
Etherial in its very ghastliness—
Or is she dead? It is the room where stands
The cabinet of olden memories,
But now not hallowed by the blessed Cross
That whilom gleamed thereon. Its angel forms,
With hands uplift in prayer, are lost i' the gloom;
But underneath, where pallid moonbeams creep,
The fiendish heads are grinning—Is she dead?

This is no tale of ordinary moan;
Of death and sweetly solemn memories
That haunt the peaceful sepulchre, and build
Upon its wormy hollowness high hopes,
Immortal aspirations. 'Tis a chant
To fill with dreary wail Hadean glooms
And wake the echoes of the vast abyss
To exultation fierce, unless 'twere sung
In heaven to heavenly harmonies, by soft

Angelic voices modulated sweet
With saintly tones of human tenderness,
In low, ineffable pleadings, it might move
Divine compassion.   No, she is not dead.
Tho' like a marble sorrow sculptured there
She sits, her face upturned amid the gloom,
White, white and cold, her lips move murmuringly,
While in half consciousness her weary thoughts
Are wandering in the past.   She whispers low,—
" Mother ! how lonely is this fearful house—
'Tis haunted, mother ! in the storm, in the night,
The Forest women came, but when they looked
Upon the silver Crucifix I wore
They fled with such dire screams that all aswoon
I fell, and when I woke could never find
My sweet Cross more.   Pray, mother, pray to God,
That he may send an angel down to seek
It o'er the world.   Or teach me how to pray—
A fearful life they lead who cannot pray
To the sweet saints !   They say I am a witch.
O mother, come to me, and let us talk
Of the old times of peace before I die."
Thus her subverted faculties, meanwhile,
Wandered, perplexed by wild unearthly fears:
But soon restored to her accustomed calm
She felt again the burden of her grief ;

She felt the mystic Presence darkening
Above her head, waiting the dreaded hour,
So fast approaching, to envelope all
Her being with its horror, shutting in
And bearing down her spirit to the abodes
Of endless wail! Yet what in those low realms
More terrible than is the torturing fear,
The freezing agony, of her suspense.

But now the end is near. The midnight moon
Scarce slants her beams through the deep oriel.
'Tis Agatha's last hour—and never more
Shall she behold those once familiar walls,
Hallowed with childhood's memories; no more
Shall gaze upon the moonbeams, white and wan
As her own face, and all as cold, as cold!
And never more shall feel the sunlight fall
Upon her golden hair, now silvery dim
In the white glimmer of the moon, and all
Wandering about her shoulders like a dream.
The hour glides on, and as it passes slow
The dreadful Presence closes round her still,
Shutting out light, and air, and consciousness
Of aught but pain and sorrow—closer yet—
Darker and more intense it gathers there—
Till in a swoon of fear she loses quite
All sense of outward being, save of THAT

Which darkens all her soul with endless night;
While deepens more the agony within,
Beneath whose weight her weary soul shall sink
To the abysmal gloom. But from this trance
Of terror she at length awakes—to what?
To find her fear a dread reality?
To find her dream a dream? This is no dream.
"Mother!" she murmurs low, as if she knew
Her mother near, as if her mother's hand
Were laid upon her hair. This is no dream.
Upon her bosom whose last pulse is faint
With the fast ebbing life, a hand is laid
That strikes through all her frame a fiery thrill
Of strange emotions sweet, consuming there
The frozen, stagnant fear; and as the glow
Of long forgotten peace, ineffable,
Sinks down, deep, deep into her desolate soul,
She lifts her weak and wavering hands in prayer,
And with a joy purer than seraphs feel
Presses unto her dying heart once more
The Cross of her Redeemer—thus restored—
But by no mortal hand! From the infinite
    heights
Of heavenly compassion had her love
And innocence this favour won, to balk
The powers of darkness and subvert the doom
Her love had dared—her innocence had borne!

Morn dawns aslant the pines with golden
    beams,
And through the antique oriel, lighting up
The cabinet of olden memories
And the winged angels with clasped hands of
    prayer.
And now it gilds the silver Crucifix
Whose crimson band runs like a ruddy vein
Around the marble neck of Agatha ;
And shines upon her sleeping face, and sheds
A glory round her hair, and o'er her form
Ethereal lustres—till her slumbers seem
More beautiful than any earthly sleep—
Yet what more earthly than the sleep of death—
Yet what more heavenly ? For upon her face,
So wondrous, wondrous fair, and on her lips,
Her poor, pale lips, the old, old smile has left
Its most ineffable meanings ! So she lies—
With her thin fingers frozen round the Cross—
In that dim room of shadowy shapes and
    dreams :
How long ? O ye, whose hearts have truly felt
The love, the pity of this legend old—
Whose memories have still some calm recess,
Sacred to the ideal forms that glide
Out of the poet's shaping phantasy—
Let that lone figure lie forever there,
With cold hands folded o'er her dreamless heart,
In the white beauty of immortal death !

THE WEIRD WOMAN.

"A sort of allegory, of a soul,
A sinful soul, possessed of many gifts."
—*Tennyson.*

I.

ONCE, in a pathless and primeval glen,
   Through which a torrent ploughed its narrow course,
And down its deep, sepulchral hollows ran,
   Plunging from rock to rock with murmurings hoarse,
   From the deep heart of Pendle, where its source
In sunless caverns with the gnomes did hide;
   There, in the passage of the mountain force,
Under the shadow of a steep hill side,
A wondrous Witch did far from human kind abide.

Her dwelling was an ancient tower, all hoar
  And massive as an old Cyclopean wall,
Built in the times unknown to mortal lore,
  By those who to their aid had dared to call
  The powers that hold the elements in thrall;
For its huge blocks by human means alone
  Were never reared; old as the hills, and all
As undecayed, though thousand storms had blown
Against its rugged sides, with grey moss overgrown.

Into this gloomy house no light could creep,
  Save by a narrow portal, seeming more
Like a deep fissure cloven in the steep
  Front of a solid rock than any door
  For human feet to pass, and from of yore,
No mortal foot the secret ways had trod
  Of that dark cell or its unhallowed floor,
Until this Witch had made it her abode,
That she might there defy the laws of man and God.

And far within the darkness there, 'tis said,
  A fearful chasm yawned, like that of old
Oracular in Delphi, where that maid,
  The Pythoness, inhaled the vapours rolled
    Out of the depths beneath, and thence foretold,

In rapt, prophetic fury, things to come!
A craggy gulf Avernian which did hold
The mysteries of Hecat and of doom,
And led through grisly shades to Pluto's realms
    of gloom.

Within this den the Sorceress dwelt, and there
    Did seek to fathom all the mysteries deep
Which give to mortals power in earth and air,
    And o'er the spirits that forever sweep
        Through stellar glooms, and o'er the gnomes that creep
Amid the elemental life below—
    And o'er the fiends! And thus she strove to heap
Forbidden lore in her proud heart, and know
The powers that sway the world and weave its
    wondrous show.

She knew the secret name of every star,
    And all their influence o'er the sons of clay;
And from their mystic motions could declare
    What destiny the powers to whom we pray
        Had pre-ordained the inevitable day:
She knew the virtues all earth's flowers do store
    Within their silken cells, and legends say
She had distilled the juice of many more,
By shadowy fingers culled on Lethe's silent shore.

In these the powers she found of spells malign,
  Of soothing anodynes, nepenthes rare,
Of opiates bland, of vaporous ethers fine,
  Whose power might with the magic herbs compare
Medea gathered in the moonlight air,—
For ere the passing years one shadow threw
  Upon the whiteness of her forehead fair,
With these she could at will her youth renew,
Her beauty, such as ne'er in mortal form we view.

Not all the powers that magic ever found
  In witch's cauldron, or Lethean pool,
Or night weeds gathered on enchanted ground,
  Each 'neath its baleful star, have that control
  Over the passions of the human soul
As heaven-born beauty hath, too oft of hell
  And hell's dark agencies the unhallowed tool
By dark subversion made, and doth avail
To lure the heart astray, when fate and folly fail.

This knew the Enchantress—and, in haughty scorn,
  Held far aloof from all the vulgar crew
Of night-hags that on winds of darkness borne
  Flock to their foul, infernal rendezvous;
  She dwelt alone, remote from mortal view,

By nobler means aiming at nobler ends,
　　Not holier, but less hateful, for she knew
Whate'er the range of human thought transcends,
To which for aye in vain the aspiring spirit tends.

Nought recked she of the herd of common men,
　　Nor upon their low fate did spend the hours
Of her strange life in that secluded glen,
　　　　Holding dark converse with the Hadean
　　　　　　powers;
　　But to her secret subterranean bowers
Those purer souls she sought to lure alone,
　　Whose daring aspiration ever towers
Above this low terrene, to them made known
The mystic wonders hid in her dark cell of stone.

These, by her potent arts enticing, she—
　　Weaving around them many a subtle spell,
By force of soul-deluding gramarye—
　　Would draw at length to her enchanted cell,
　　To their bewildered senses would reveal
The splendours of her beauty, mystic bright,
　　A loveliness whose marvels none may tell,
Filling the tranced soul with strange delight,
And sweet ideal love, and longings infinite!

And when this failed, as sometimes it might be,
  To win them to her dark, imperious sway,
She would unto their spell-bound phantasy
  Visions of beauty and of power display
  From ages past, or worlds that far away
Beyond the great star-kingdoms ever rise,
    Or lead them through the underworld, where they
Forgot earth, air and overarching skies,
Wandering for evermore through dead eternities.

And thus abode, in solitary pride,
  The Witch, communing with her own deep mind,
In which were treasured all the marvels wide
  Of space, and time and being unconfined,
  And she would summon, by her arts refined,
The wandering sprites wherever they might be,
  Who to her bidding came on every wind
And did her errands over land and sea,
Or to the sunless bourne of drear immensity!

II.

Who cometh through the Forest from afar?
   A youth, with aspect pale and eager eye
That gleams beneath his dark hair like the star
   On which he gazes in the western sky.
   " Lead me, oh, lead me thither, ere I die,
Bright symbol of the element divine
   That burns within me, my mortality,
Consuming all, until this soul of mine
Shall seek its kindred spheres, with them and
     thee to shine."

"What seekest thou in Pendle's haunted bound?"
   "O wandering voice, I may not answer thee!"
" Avaunt, avaunt, from this enchanted ground!"
   " O threatening voices, not the furies three,
   Nor all the region powers shall baffle me."
" Come hither, hither! fear not, come away!"
   " O sweet, O soft, æolian melody,
That would my weary footsteps lead astray,
The goal before me lies, I cannot, dare not stay."

THE WEIRD WOMAN. 297

A rocky path leads up the mountain glen—
  Way-weary wanderer hast thou strength to climb?
Oh, what are rocks of adamant to men
  Whose souls are formed for destinies sublime!
  In the still hour of placid eventime,
With bleeding feet, and wild dishevelled hair,
  Before that house, all hoar with ages' rime,
He stands alone, while Hesper, large and fair,
Throbs like a heart of fire down through the twilight air.

He stands alone and panting—from his breast
  Draws forth a Scroll, where, in each mystic line,
Unutterable meanings are expressed,
  Secrets that make humanity divine!
  And thus he spake:—" By every sacred sign,
That here revealeth what to mortals may
  Be spoken never—ere yon star decline
Behind the summit of the mountain grey,
Come forth! the spell I use thou canst not disobey."

He held the Scroll aloft, and pointed still
  Unto the sinking star, which even then
Trembled upon the verge of the dark hill;
  But ere it sunk behind it, from her den
    The Witch came forth—fierce as a tigress when

Rushing upon her foes, she threatening flies
    To seize the Scroll, and it perforce had ta'en,
But the youth stood erect with dauntless eyes
And with unshaken grasp her utmost power defies.

Her mightiest charms of no avail he knew
    While still he held that mystic Scroll secure ;
And though, all fiercely beautiful, she grew
    A gorgon dread, with snaky locks impure,
        And threatening terrors thronged the air, obscure
With preternatural gloom, and every sound
    Of fear assailed him, he did all endure ;
And when her dark spells passed he looked around,—
And, lo,—a woman kneeling, weeping on the ground !

And she was beautiful beyond compare,
    Beyond all mortal beauty beautiful ;
Beneath the shadow of her floating hair
    Her white breasts heaved like waves beneath the full,
White moon; no shape marmoreal,
By god-like sculptor carved, was half so fair :
    Beyond all mortal moan ineffable,
The passion of her eyes uplifted there,
Dark, fathomless, forlorn, as her divine despair

And when she spoke her voice was like a dream
  Of love in some far world, remote, and mild,
And lone, and lovely, such as poets deem,
  Where Echo mourns her sorrows to the wild,
  And wandering spirits, from heavenly spheres exiled,
Sing, floating down the hollow vast of night :
  "Thou hast prevailed, O gifted, glorious child :
I know not what thou art, or by what right
Thou dost usurp my star, my power, my love, my light,

My very soul." She stood erect and calm,
  And yielded up to him her wand of spells—
"Receive thou this, dread stranger, as the palm
  Of thy great victory o'er her who dwells
  Remote from man in subterranean cells;
Whate'er above or underneath may be
  Obeys her strong enchantment, that compels
All other power in earth, or air, or sea—
All things submit to her who now submits to thee."

Silent the stranger stood—filling his heart
  With her ethereal beauty, whereunto
The touch of human sorrow did impart
    A power her proud defiance never knew
    Spirits of loftiest nature to subdue ;

Of what avail, when 'neath that touch her own
    Strong will was broken? Silently he drew
The Enchantress now towards that cell of stone,
Where she no more must dwell amidst her spells
    alone.

And as they paused before the portal dim,
    She murmured low,—"My spirits, ye are free!
Ye, who through ocean's heaving vastness swim,
    And build your coral bowers beneath the sea;
Who in the cavernous earth work silently;
Who dance upon the lonely moonlit wold;
    Who flit like light from star to star, and ye
Who dwell amidst Hadean shadows old,
Beyond the utmost bourne of Lethe, dark and
    cold.

"No more shall ye obey my dread commands—
    On eager pinions shall ye speed no more,
To bring me gems and gold from distant lands,
    From distant realms mysterious treasures pour
    At my proud feet—the hidden paths explore
Of nature and of supernatural things;
    Revealing secrets that no human lore
Dreams ever in its dark imaginings,
No prophet shadows forth, no sacred poet sings.

"My empire over you is passed away —
The wide dominions my imperious mind
Did from its secret throne of spells survey,
 By no dark doubts or shadowy fears confined,
 Whose intimate intelligence combined
The present with the future and the past,
 Wherein I dwelt apart from human kind,
My faery realms, so beautiful and vast,
Are vanished like a dream, from which I wake at last,

"To what I know not; knowing this alone,—
 That I who felt not mortal hope nor fear,
Who, far from human sympathies, had grown
  Proud, strong and self-sustained, stand trembling here
 In doubt and dread of what may next appear
To shake into the dust my ruined pride."
 She spoke, and turned towards the wanderer,
And through the dark and narrow porch they glide,
While night descends o'er all that region wild and wide.

And through the stillness of the starlit air
 These voices float, from hill, stream, rock and tree,—
"Spirits, rejoice, the Woman, dread and fair,
 Restores us to our ancient liberty."
  'Away, away, upon the winds so free!"

"Down to the caverns where the Titans dwell."
"Back to old Nereus, his children we!"
"And we to the Pandean woods." "Farewell! The wand has lost its power, and silent is the spell."

III.

Upon a throne of amethyst and gold
  The Enchantress sat ; and round her might be seen
Splendours of starlit gems, and treasures old,
  And silver shapes, and essences serene ;
  All lovely things that in the world have been,
Or in its dreams ; and over all there fell
  A glamour as of moonlight's pearliest sheen ;
Earth-fuming incense filled that faery cell,
And Pan made music there, tuned to the sea-god's shell.

As one ashamed of all her lonely state
  And selfish pride she sat, while at her feet
Reclined the youth, with earnest eyes, sedate
  And full of sorrow, full of passion sweet,
  While in low, pleading tones he thus did greet
That Weird Woman :—"Queen of this bright bower !
Oh, yet awhile retain thy radiant seat,
Let me behold thee on thy throne of power,
In all the matchless grace of thy serenest hour.

"Knowest thou not, then," she said, in mournful
    tone,
  "My beauty only with my power may last;—
That all my being hung on that alone—
    And seest thou not they both are waning fast,
    Now that my magic arts have from me passed?
And yet for what life has been mourn not I,
    But what it might have been." The youth,
        aghast,
Started from where he sat—"Must thou, too,
    die?
And is it thus we share each other's destiny?

"For mine own death I was prepared alone;
    Yet for myself did hope, and will for thee:—
The Scroll, the mystic Scroll! Its teachings
        known,
    We yet may find the secret that shall be
    A spell of life-renewing potency.
List! until briefly I to thee have told
    My story, full of doom and mystery,
And, as the purposes of fate unfold,
    Let us remain through all fearless, and calm and
        bold.

"Know that I too with loftiest aims have striven,
    Apart from human sympathies have stood,
Seeking the power by knowledge only given;
    At midnight's starry prime 'twas mine to brood
    O'er secrets which the mighty dead have wooed

Out of the dull, unconscious depths of fate;
   Like thee, forbidden paths have I pursued
Beyond the limits of our mortal state,
Into the formless void of essence increate!

"Thus in my intellectual pride alone
   I dwelt, by mortal wishes unsubdued;
For all the powers of life to me were known,
   Or so I deemed, when to my solitude
     There came an ancient hermit, mild and good;
The stately man with grave majestic look,
   Calm and inscrutable before me stood;
And, bearing in his hand this wondrous Book,
With slow, oracular voice the solemn silence broke.

"'Proud searcher of the mysteries of life,
   Explorer of the paths of destiny,
Aspirer after powers by which its strife
   With the material elements may be
     Thought's rugged path to immortality!
Thou knowest much, and much unknown remains,
   Of secrets that no mortal eye doth see,
Save when the Power that rules the world ordains,
And not the least of these this sacred Book contains.

"'If thou would'st read the secret written here,
   Renounce thy magic arts, nor dwell alone;
Seek thou the distant Forest, wild and drear,
   Seek the Weird Woman in her cave of stone!
When she its mighty influence too shall own,
Then read—and learn the destiny divine,
   Else to your proud, impassive hearts unknown
For evermore.'—Henceforth the Scroll was mine,—
And earnestly I gazed upon each mystic line.

"In vain—my knowledge nought availed me then,
   And yet an influence from the Book there came,
That led me forth among the homes of men;
   My power renounced, forgotten all my fame,
Again I felt the feeling and the flame
Of human love and pity for mankind.
   As I still wandered on, I heard thy name—
And from that moment, with impetuous mind,
I sought through dangerous paths thy secret haunts to find.

"'Through dangerous paths, through forests terror-haunted,
   Unaided by mine art, alone I passed!
And though the ardent spirit was undaunted,
   My mortal strength began to fail at last:
I felt that life was ebbing from me fast,

When these grey hills rose darkly on my view:
   The rest thou knowest—how with desperate haste
I called thee forth, and o'er thy spirit too
The Scroll's mysterious power wrought feelings strange and new.

"My strength begins to fail— my tale is o'er—
   Let us the charmèd words together read,
Whose power our fainting souls may yet restore,
   To human life and love our spirits lead ;
Or whatsoever doom he there decreed,
Haste we to know it, Being bright and fair ;
   I would not from its dread control be freed,
If I with thee the future still may share,
As thus beside thee now its unknown powers I dare !"

Thus speaking, he unfurled the mighty Book,
   And then upon its writing mystical,
All eagerly and pale, with fixed look,
   They gazed. And, lo ! the fading splendours fell
Into deep darkness through that silent cell :
Save that a faint, white lustre lingers where
   Those twain so beautiful, by some strong spell
O'er-mastered, still upon that writing stare,
With eager eyes to read the heavenly secret there.

And still they gaze, with blank yet wistful eyes,
   On characters all darkly sybiline—
Until, at length, a gleam of glad surprise
   Doth in their eyes and on their faces shine;—
   And still they read—and as they read entwine
Their arms around each other lovingly!
   Then, with a smile of rapturous joy, divine,
They look upon each other and so die—
And darkness like a shroud enfolds them
   peacefully!

It may be in the guise of hermit grey,
   That some kind saint took pity on those twain,
Who in forbidden paths had gone astray,
   And from pursuits so perilous and vain
   Thus led them back to hope and peace again,
By the soft touch of human sympathy;
   It may be that that writing did contain
A spell so sacred sweet that they must die
To read and understand its heavenly mystery!

The legend sayeth not—but this is sure,
   That when the morning on those mountains
      grey
Arose, and slanted down that glen obscure
   The pale effulgence of its earliest ray,
   The dwelling of the Witch had passed away,

And nought was there save heaps of mossy
    stone,
  O'er which the streamlet dashed its snowy
    spray,
That to the quiet hills maketh its moan,
Whose lonely rocks since then no other sound
    have known.

So must it ever be that whosoe'er
  In solitude would dwell above mankind,
Seeking alone to know the supreme fair,
  And in imaginary realms would find,
  Or in the pure abstractions of the mind,
Humanity's sole solace and delight,
  Rebels against the heavenly powers, who bind
The meanest atom to the infinite,
And on the poorest weed shower down celestial
    light.

And though they build their speculative towers
  High o'er the human throngs that toil below,
And proudly revel in ideal bowers,
  Where the strong gusts of passion never blow;
  Indifferent to human weal or woe :
Yet when their high-raised thought shall reach
    the skies,
  A touch, a breath, its pride shall overthrow,
Even from the meanest impulse they despise,
And nature vindicate her holiest energies.

FRAGMENTS.

"Some waif, washed up with the strays and spars,
Which ebbtide shows to the shore and the stars.
Weed from the water, grass from a grave,
A broken blossom, a ruined rhyme."

—Swinburne.

DARK MORNINGS.

I LOVE not more the golden dawns of spring
  Than these dark mornings of the year's decline,
These grey November mornings, when day's orb,
As though unwillingly he left the skies
Of happier climes, slow rises with a frown.
Nor do I cease to frequent my old walks,
My old, loved walks, to watch the gradual light
Kindle the dawn, quenching the stellar fires,
Till heaven is void, except for some lone star
Whose silver ray upon the horizon's rim
Intensely trembles; or where overhead,
Supremely calm, the flaming Jupiter
Steadies his bright car in the midst of heaven!

* * * * *

THE MOON.

"What is there in thee, moon, that thou should'st move
My heart so potently?"
Keats.

* * *

AND thus I stood in spirit worshipping,
While the swift dark did silently uprear
In starry spaces night's unmeasured dome,
A temple huge, and worthy to be hallowed
By so serene a presence ; thus I gazed,
Enamoured of that supreme loveliness,
Till my heart owned the idolatry of old
That builded glorious fanes to that fair moon,
As to a beautiful goddess, with white robes,
And silver bow, and arrows glittering keen,
Celestial guardian of all pure thoughts,
And naming her the Chastity of heaven !

Or did a human sympathy inspire
That face, so sad in its tranquillity
As though some angel, from his sphery guard
Down stooping, sorrowed o'er a world of woe?

* * * * *

                      Oh, whatsoe'er
Imagination feigned to recognise
In that impassive countenance serene,
My heart still worshipped, worshipped even with
    tears,
That heavenly symbol, that uplifted ark,
The unveiled shekinah of a mystic Power,
The divine Tenderness, the essential Love,
That zones eternity.

* * * * *

GREETINGS.

* * *

THOU wert a wanderer on the hills, my friend;
　　The "power of hills" was on thee, and
　　　　the power
Of the great poet, him of Rydal Mere.
To thee the noble books, the kingly bards,
To thee "the far-off ways of light," were known.
Of such as thou were Yorick and Eugene—
Bear greetings to the "far celestial land!"

ADMER:
A MYSTERY.

"Thou shalt know the mystic song
Chanted when the sphere was young."
—*Emerson*.

WHERE is Admer, the beautiful child?
    Moaneth his mother by night and day,
And his sisters kneel in the church and pray
For the dear little brother, so gentle and mild,
    Whom the weird Woman has stolen away.

*   *   *   *

On a lonely moor, so pathless and dim,
    In a lonely house, in a lonely room,
    Admer is reading a Book of Doom,
And over the Book, and over him,
    There stands a Woman, wondrous fair,
    And her eyes are as stars in the twilight air,

And her voice is sweet, as she whispers low
   The words of an unknown tongue, the lore
Of the Book, she has brought him there to know,
   The speech he must learn to speak before
He can talk with her and her friends: and soon
Admer can read the mystic Rune.

       *   *   *   *

" Who are these that come and go,
   In the still rooms and the garden there,
   Among the roses and lilies fair,
Down in the wood where the sunsets glow?
   Do they talk to the trees of things unknown?
   Do they walk with spirits, or walk alone?"
And the Woman weird made answer slow,
" Admer, thy time is come to know."

And she led him forth in the garden fair,
And a wild-eyed boy, with shining hair,
   Came to him and greeted him rapturously:
   " Admer, my brother, we welcome thee!
   Thou shalt learn a heavenly mystery.
Our sister, the Witch, whom the dark world fears
And hates, as it hated us in the years
   When I and my brothers abode with men,
   Has taught thee the lore she taught us then,

When she brought us away from the servile
    throng,
Who flatter the cunning and toil for the strong.
  Thou art one of us!" And there came a crowd
  Of happy children, who sang aloud :
" We were the victims of falsehood and fear,
Till the weird Woman brought us here
  To the lonely house on the moorland lone,
  To the garden and wood where we live with
    our own."

And they led him away in the woodland old,
Where a mystic Child, with a harp of gold,
  Was singing to himself alone
  A song the world has never known.
And the words were the words of the Book of
    Doom,
Which the children read in the lonely room,
  Taught by the Woman to sing and say,
  The weird Woman who stole them away ;
And the music sweet only they may hear
Who have followed her footsteps without fear ;
  And the meaning divine no bard can tell
  In the language of men who buy and sell ;
For the song is the song of the angels seven,
And the strings of the harp are the stars of
    heaven !

And into the forest there came a Knight,
All armed in steel, as glittering bright
  As the bright, blue fire of the summer star,
  And his voice was a trumpet that called to war,
That called to war for the children dear,
Who are held in the bondage of falsehood and fear.
  And Admer heard it, and said, " Shall I go
  With the steel-clad Knight against his foe ? "
" His foe and mine," said the Woman weird ;
" Follow the Knight ! and be not afeard."
  And she gave him a sword of steel and gold,
  Which she had brought from an armoury old,
" For the sake of the children, take this with thee,
And follow the Knight who will set them free
In the name of the heavenly mystery ! "

NOTES.

NOTE 1, PAGE 17.

'*The Song of Brun.*'

The Brun, or Burn, which gives its name to Burnley, rises on the moors beyond Hurstwood and Extwistle, and flows through scenes of great natural beauty, in the neighbourhood of which many remains of Roman and prehistoric times have been discovered.

NOTE 2, PAGE 155.

'*Loch Achray.*'

This and the following piece are memorials of a short visit to the Trossachs and the neighbouring Highlands, in May, 1877. The view of Ben Venue over the loch is very fine, and had the effect of inspiring one of my companions, who, either from emulation or in a spirit of ridicule, composed the following quatrain, on the spot.

  O Ben Venue! O Ben Venue!
   I've heard of you severest strictur',
  I thought you was a reg'lar do,
   But now I find—you're like my pictur'!

NOTE 3, PAGE 162.

'*A Quartette.*'

This poem refers to a certain Quixotic journey, or tramp, to London in 1866, an account of which appeared in the *Burnley Advertiser*, and was published the year following in booklet form under the title "From Lancashire to London on Foot." The "quartette" were my friends Dr. Dean, Mr. Joshua Rawlinson, Mr. Thomas Nowell and myself. Our travelling names, as I may call them—"The Duke," "The General," "The Lieutenant," and "Mine Ancient," were taken from *The Merchant of Venice*, but have no reference to anything in the play. They were simply used as a convenient mode of referring to certain personal characteristics and incidents of the journey. "Knotgrass," (page 36) is a reminiscence of the same journey.

NOTE 4, PAGE 166.

'*On a certain Poem, &c.*'

The poem here referred to will be found in "Local Rhymes," published in 1890, by my old friend, Mr. Henry Nutter.

NOTE 5, PAGE 172.

'*A Memory, &c.*'

Burnley is not without its high historic associations. It is now generally admitted (see Craik, Grossart, and other authorities) that Spenser's visit to the "North country," in 1574, was to Hurstwood, or some of the neighbouring homesteads of the Spenser clan. For the wanderings of George Fox—"my unfortunate George!" (Carlyle)— through the Pendle country and over the top of Pendle Hill, in the year 1652, see "George Fox's Journal," Sewel's "History of the people called Quakers," and James Mackay's "Pendle Hill in History and Literature."

These historic memories are woven into another web in the "Forest Dream" (page 25), together with Wordsworth's recognition of Pendle Hill from Norton Tower in "The White Doe of Rylstone."

NOTE 6, PAGE 176.

'*A Cenotaph.*'

This piece was written for one of the "Penny Readings" given in connection with the Mechanics' Institution, on the 21st April, 1864.

NOTE 7, PAGE 184.

'*A Rhyme of Jubilee.*'

The Jubilee for which this rhyme was composed was held in the first week in January, 1883, to celebrate the fiftieth anniversary of the founding of the Mechanics' Institution. The names of the four working men who "well and truly laid" the corner stone of this noble institution, in the shape of a cottage library in the "Meadows," were William Wood, Thomas Booth, — Yates and — Leeming, all employed at Marsland's foundry.

"They did good work that will endure,
  They laid the strong foundations sure."

ERRATA.

Preface, page xii, line 16, *delete* "last," and read "*the two sections entitled, &c.*"

Page 15, line 8, for "voice," read "*voices*,"
"And the voices of women and men who prayed."

Page 162, line 3, for "your," read "*four*,"
"By four most famous wights."

Page 189, line 15, for "oar," read "*car*," line 17, for "this," read "*his*."

Page 278, line 22, for "chattering," read "*chatterings*."

THE COMMITTEE.

JOSHUA RAWLINSON, J.P., *Chairman*.
FRED. J. GRANT, J.P.
J. LANGFIELD WARD, M.A.
ALFRED STRANGE, J.P.
ALDERMAN GREENWOOD, J.P.
W. LEWIS GRANT.
REV. T. LEYLAND.
T. BROWN, M.D., J.P.
JAMES KAY, J.P.
FRED. H. HILL.
JAS. LANCASTER.
W. LANCASTER, JUNR.
W. THOMPSON.
H J. ROBINSON, B.A., M.R.C.S.
W. T. FULLALOVE.
J. WHITTAKER, J.P. (NELSON).
HENRY NUTTER.
TATTERSALL WILKINSON.
J. W. KNEESHAW.
P. J. ROBERTS, F.G.S.
T. BOOTH.
J. BRADSHAW.
G. HINDLE.
J. GORDON.
ROBT. RADCLIFFE.
COUN. W. E. HACKING.
WM. SMITHSON.
W. GRIME.
S. AUSTERBERRY.
F. C. LONG.
M. TATTERSALL.
J. VANN.
L. HEAP.
J. CROOK.

    T. G. CRUMP, B.A., M.B., ⎱ *Hon. S*
    JOHN ALLEN, ⎰

LIST OF SUBSCRIBERS.

	VOLS.
Aitken, James, Spring Grove, Barrowford	1
Allen, Helen, 24, Queensberry Road ...	1
Allen, John, 24, Queensberry Road	1
Alston, Albert, 9, Grimshaw Street	1
Altham, Councillor J. L., Beechwood...	1
Altham, P. H., Beechwood ...	1
Anningson, Dr. Thirkell, 111, Cleethorpe Road, Grimsby ...	1
Armistead, Alderman William, 61, Colne Road	1
Ashworth, Ashworth, 41, Danes House Road	1
Ashworth, Edwin, 6, Sackville Street	1
Ashworth, James, 33, Bridge Street	1
Ashworth, William, Centre, Nelson	1
Aspinall, William, 108, Todmorden Road...	1
Austerberry, Stocks, 65, Curzon Street	1
Balderston, W., 128, Railway Terrace, Padiham	1
Baldwin, Councillor John, Hazel Mount	1
Bardsley, Isaac, 96, Mount Pleasant Street, Oldham	1
Barlow, Joseph A., 1, Accrington Road	1
Barnes, John, 14, Rosehill Terrace	1
Baron, Arthur, 193, Manchester Road	1
Baron, Alderman John, J.P., 179, Manchester Road	1
Barrett, Councillor Charles, Yorkshire Street	1
Bayne, Councillor Thomas, Ighten Grange	1
Beecham, Harry, 33, Brunswick Street	1
Beecham, Richard, 62, Crowther Street	1
Bell, Edward, 25, Fair View Road	1
Bell, Thomas, 43, Ormerod Road	1
Bell, J. J. Howard, M.I.J., *Express Office*	1
Berry, E., 1, Helena Street ...	1
Berry, James, Brookside	2
Berry, William, Commercial Hotel, Coal Street	1
Bibby, Councillor Jas., 24, Westgate	1
Birnie, J., 81, Todmorden Road ...	1
Bond, D., County Police Station, Bank Parade	1
Booth, Thomas, 19, Plover Street	1

Booth, William, 5, Ferguson Street, Halifax   1
Boys, Richard, St. James' Street...   1
Bradley, John, Sunnyholme...   1
Bradshaw, John, 42, Yorkshire Street...   1
Bradshaw, Richard, Market Place   1
Brierley, Wynford, Carr Road, Nelson   1
Brotherton, H., 3, St. James' Row   1
Brotherton, Lawrence, 7, Ormerod Road   1
Broughton, Robert, 23, Market Street   1
Brown, John, M.D., J.P., Bank Parade   1
Brown, J., 29, Ormerod Road   1
Brown, James, 416, Colne Road   1
Brumbley, Charles, 58, Master Street...   1
Bulcock, Henry, Manchester Road   1
Burgess, Henry, 58, Manchester Road   1
Burnett, W. H., Brae Side, Blackburn   1
Burnley Church Institute   1
Burnley Co-operative Society   2
Burnley Mechanics' Institution   2
Burrows, Alderman, J.P., Ashleigh, Colne Road   1
Burrows, B., Bookseller, Burnley Wood Post Office   1
Butler, Edwin, 24, Gisburne Road, Barrowford   1
Butterfield, John, 41, Ormerod Road...   1
Butterworth, John, J.P., Oak Bank   6
Butterworth, S., 57, Todmorden Road   1

Campbell, S., "Fighting Cocks Inn," Mereclough   1
Carrington, Councillor Albert, 65, Ormerod Road   1
Chadwick, Hitchon, L.R.C.P., L.R.C.S, 43, Oxford Road...   1
Chadwick, Wm., 71, Colne Road   1
Chew, John, 24, Holme Road   1
Chew, William, 32, Aqueduct Street   1
Clark, Henry, 169, Woodside   1
Clement, Leonard, Forest Villa, Nelson   1
Collinge, James, St. James' Street   1
Collinge, J. S., J.P., Park House   3
Collinge, Alderman W., J.P.   3
Cooke, Thomas, 152, Colne Road   1
Cooke, Samuel, 5, Carlton Road...   1
Cornish, J. E., Bookseller, 16, St. Ann's Square, Manchester   1
Coulston, William, Bookseller, Victoria Buildings   3
Coupe, Edward, 7, Siddall Street, Hopwood, Heywood...   1
Cowell, J., 56, St. James' Street...   2
Cowell, William, Orchard Place...   1

Cowgill, Bryan, 48, Manchester Road ... 1
Crawshaw, E., 9, Tollington Park, London, N. 1
Cronkshaw's Hotel, Burnley 1
Cronkshaw, John, Alden, Merlin Road, Revidge,
    Blackburn 1
Crook, Campbell, 64, Albion Street ... 1
Crook, James, 23, Townley Street ... 1
Crook, Thomas, 132, Manchester Road 1
Crossley, Arthur, Carlton Road 1
Crump, T. G., B.A., M.B., 62, Prospect Terrace 1
Cunliffe, Thomas, 33, Co-operation Street, Bacup 1

Davies, Rev. T. R., 10, Ormerod Road 1
Davies, T., Bookseller, 86, Manchester Road, Nelson 1
Dean, John, 12, Smalley Street 1
Dean, Thomas, M.D., 84, Manchester Road ... 1
Dickinson, Councillor D. D., 39, Trafalgar Road 1
Dickinson, Alderman Wm., J.P., Palatine Square 2
Duckett, James, J.P., Woodleigh 1
Duckworth, Joshua, 20, St. Matthew's Street ... 1
Dunkerley, V., 87, Todmorden Road... ... 1

Eastwood, J. W., 27, Rowley Street 1
Easton, William, 28, St. James' Street 1
Edmondson, Allan, 23, Thurston Street . 1
Edmondson, John M., 14, Yorkshire Street 1
Edmundson, Marmaduke, 59, Rectory Road 1
Ellershaw, John, 14, Waterloo Avenue, Blackpool .. 1
Emmott, Councillor H., 9, Knightsbridge Grove 1
Evans, William, 144, Parkinson Street ... 1

Farrer, W. T., 1, Brooklands Avenue 1
Foden, C. M., J.P., Sefton Terrace 1
Forrest, A. J., Barcroft Hall ... 1
Foster, George, Yorkshire Street... . 1
Foulds, Geo. Hy., 69, Tarleton Street 1
Folds, James, Brunshaw 1
Fox, S. C , *South Wales Echo*, Cardiff 1
Fullalove, W. T., Olive Mount 1

Gill, George, Woodleigh ... 2
Gledhill, Joseph, 1, Hunsle Street 1
Golden, M. D., Fair View Road 1
Gordon, Joseph, Scar Cottage . 1
Graham, W. W., 99, St. James' Street 1
Grant, Arthur, 14, Palatine Square 1
Grant, F. J., J.P., Bank Field 6

Grant, Wm. Lewis, 24, Carlton Road. 2
Gray, N. P., J.P., Healey Grove... 1
Gray, Robert, M.I.J., 20, Tabor Street 1
Greenwood, Alderman James, J.P., Manchester Road 4
Greenwood, Joseph, 192, Padiham Road ... 1
Grime, Wm., 42, Williams Road... ... 1
Grocott, Ralph, 8, Hammerton Street... 1
Gutteridge, J. D., 85, Rectory Road ... 1

Hacking, Councillor W. E., 7, Hufling Lane... 1
Hall, William, 147, Accrington Road... ... 1
Halliwell, William E., 10, Market Street ... 1
Halstead, A, *Blackpool Times*, Blackpool ... 1
Halstead, J., 8, Rectory Road 1
Halstead, Lawrence, 3, Burnley Road, Worsthorne... 1
Handsley, Robert, J.P., Reedley Lodge ... 1
Hargreaves, Henry, Albion Terrace 1
Hargreaves, W. Carey, J.P., Bankfield Villa 6
Harrison, Ben, Curzon Street 1
Harrison, J. Dilworth, Manchester Road ... 1
Harrop, Joseph, 96, Manchester Road.. 1
Hartley, James, 1a, Ormerod Road ... 1
Hartley, J. T., 22, Nelson Square 1
Hartley, R., J.P., 62, Colne Road 1
Hartley, Thomas, Livery Stables, Church Street 1
Hartley, William, Thorn Hill 3
Harwood, T. H., M.D., Wilfield House 1
Haslam, T., Healey Mount 1
Hayes, B., 159, St. James' Street 1
Healey, T., 15, Orlands Rd., Clapham, London, S.W. 1
Heap, Frederick, 172, Todmorden Road 1
Heap, James, 45, Colne Road .. 1
Heap, Lawrence, 110, New Hall Street 1
Heaton, Mrs. M. A., 99, Rectory Road 1
Heys, G., 49, Manchester Road, Hapton 1
Heys, Nathan, Arcade, Colne .. 1
Hey, W. H., Hazel Mount, Nelson 1
Hill, Fred H., Thorn Hill 4
Hindle, George, 22, Gillowe Street 1
Hinton, J., 36, Calder Vale Road 1
Hirst, Thos., J.P., Ashfield House 1
Hodgson, J., L.R.C.P., L.R.C.S., Gannow Lane 1
Hodkin, George, 5, Ormerod Road ... 1
Holden, Samuel, 38, Accrington Road 1
Holgate, James, 1, Albert Street... 1
Holgate, Thomas, 23, Colne Road 1
Holmes, Councillor D., J.P., 43, Bankhouse Street . 1

Holmes, J. P., 22, Regent Street, Bacup — 1
Holmes, James, 35, Murray Street ... — 1
Holt, R. C., F.R.C.S., Byerden House — 1
Hopwood, W. T., 103, Castle Street ... — 1
Horn, J. S., Palatine Square ... ... — 1
Horne, J. H., M.I.J., 72, Belvedere Road ... — 1
Horner, Mrs., 54, Rectory Road... — 1
Houlding, Edward, Central Mill... ... ... — 4
Howard, Wm. R., London and Midland Bank, Ltd. — 1
Howarth, George, 100, Hollingreave Road ... — 1
Howker, Enoch, 62, Leyland Road ... — 1
Howker, Percy, 68, Belvedere Road ... ... — 1
Howorth, John, J.P., Park View ... ... — 1
Hudson, J., 95, Spencer Place, Leeds ... — 1
Hudson, Sam., 17, Bridge Street... — 1

Jackson, Thomas, Junr., L.D.S., 23, Hargreaves Street — 1
Jee, Charles, 91, Manchester Road ... ... — 2
Jobling, A., 59, Ormerod Road ... ... — 1
Johnson, Edwin, Manchester Road ... ... — 1
Jones, Edward, 70, Prospect Terrace ... ... — 1
Judson, Timothy, 71, Church Street ... ... — 1

Kay, James, J.P., Towneley Villa ... ... — 12
Kay-Shuttleworth, The Right Hon. Sir U. J., Bart.,
    M.P., Gawthorpe Hall ... ... — 1
Keighley, Alderman G., J.P., Woodfield House — 1
Keighley, Gilbert, 25-27, Nicholas Street ... — 1
Keighley, Samuel, 25-27, Nicholas Street .. — 1
Kneeshaw, J. W., 31, Todmorden Road ... — 1

Lancaster, Alderman Alfred, J.P., Fern Bank — 4
Lancaster, James, 27, Carlton Road ... ... — 1
Lancaster, William, Junr., 25, Carlton Road — 4
Landless, Thomas, Colliery Office — 1
Latham, Norman, 216, Colne Road — 1
Lawson, Fielden, 2, Newton Street — 1
Leaver, Arthur, 1, Broughton Street — 1
Lee, J. R., Spring Terrace, Habergham — 1
Leeming, John, 16, Thursby Road — 1
Leyland, Rev. T., Oldham — 1
Long, Frank C., 6, Plover Street — 1
Lonsdale, John, Manchester Road, Nelson — 1
Lord, Amos, 10, Newton Stree — 1
Lord, E., 5, Albion Street ... ... — 1
Lord, Lawrence, 66, Devonshire Road — 1
Lord, William, Accrington Road... — 1

Lupton, Albert, Holme View 1
Lupton, Arthur, Holly Mount 1
Lupton, Joseph T., Carlton Road 1
Lupton, Alderman W., J.P., Trafalgar House ... 2

Mackenzie, James, M.D., Bank Parade 2
Mackie, John S., 79, Coal Clough Lane 1
Maxwell, Thomas, 3, Rosemount Terrace, Newchurch 1
McCandlish, A. Stones, Cornholme 1
McCullough, James, Greeley, Colorado, U.S.A. ... 1
McFarlane, Councillor S., Holme View 1
Metcalfe, Councillor George, 120, Colne Road... ... 1
Middleton, William, 60, Heath Street 1
Miles, Rev. H. P., Lyndhurst, New Jersey, U.S.A. 1
Mitchell, Alderman C., J.P. (Mayor) 4
Mitchell, Hy., 12, Clegg Street 1
Monk, Josiah, Brookfoot Farm, Padiham 1
Moore, Benjamin, J.P., 20, Palatine Square ... 5
Moore, Isaac, 7, Briercliffe Road... 1
Moss, Rev. R. Waddy, Didsbury College 1
Mozley, Henry, 432, Colne Road 1

Nevins, W. J., 66, Coal Clough Lane ... 1
Nightingale, William, Shakespeare Terrace 1
Norman, Edwin, Knightsbridge Grove ... 1
Nowell, Thomas, Healey Grange 6
Nutter, Henry, Darwin House, Colne Road 6

Ogden, George C., Thorn Hotel 1
O'Hagan, Lady, Towneley Hall 12
Oldham, John, 112, Parkinson Street... 1

Parker, W. H., 21, Portland Street, Nelson 1
Parkinson, Alderman W., J.P., Clevelands 1
Phillips, J. W., J.P., Brown Hill 1
Pickles, I. F., 2, Oxford Road 1
Pickup, Peter, 40, Westgate... 1
Pletts, J., Borough Brewery... 1
Pomfret, Thomas, 28, Wilfield Terrace 4
Pollard, Thomas, 10, Bankhouse Street 1
Preston, Thomas, 92, Manchester Road 1
Pritchard, Thomas, 18, Palatine Square 1
Procter, Richard, Oak Mount, Westgate 1
Proctor, John, 45, Rectory Road... 1

Race, Joseph, J.P., 12, Nelson Square 1
Radcliffe, Robert, 11, Accrington Road 1
Ramsbottom, William, 4, Helena Street 1

Rawcliffe, G. B., The Sycamores.. 1
Rawcliffe, James Hawkins, Manchester Road .. 1
Rawlinson, Joshua, J.P., Oak Bank 12
Riley, Holden, 53, Ormerod Road 2
Roberts, Councillor T. H., Brooklands Avenue... 1
Roberts, P. E., Ethendune, Nelson 1
Roberts, P. J., F.G.S., Bacup 1
Robinson, Arthur, 53, Langham Street, Blackburn. 1
Robinson, H. J., B.A., M.R.C.S., Hargreaves Street... 2
Robinson, James H., L.R.C.P. & S.(ED.), 1, Carr Road, Nelson 1
Robinson, John, 134, Accrington Road 1
Robinson, Sarah Ann, 1, Gawthorpe Street, Padiham 1
Robinson, Rev. W., Woodleigh 1
Robinson, W. Parker, 138, Accrington Road 2
Routh, Thomas, 71, Parkinson Street... 1
Rycroft, John, 92, Every Street, Nelson 1

Sandy, T. G., Junr., Limefield, Brierfield 1
Scott, George, 70, Burnley Road, Bacup ... 1
Scowby, Francis, Craven Bank 1
Senior, Prof., Queen's College, Galway, Ireland 2
Shepherd, James, 56, Leyland Road 1
Simpson, Robert, Rose Cottage ... 3
Slater, Joseph, 39, St. James' Street 1
Slater, William, Woodnook 2
Smeed, Sidney, M.I.J., 28, Byerden Street... 1
Smith, A. H., Red Lion Street 1
Smith, James, Highfield Terrace ... 1
Smith, James, 6, Brougham Street 1
Smith, J. R., Padiham District Council Office . 1
Smith, John, 64, Ainsworth Street, Blackburn ... 1
Smith, Thomas, 122, Hollingreave Road 1
Smith, T. P., 9, Manchester Road ... 1
Smithson, J. B., Temperance Hotel, Leyburn, Wensleydale 1
Smithson, William, 98, Belvedere Road 2
Southern, Walter, Palace House . . 6
Spencer, Samuel, 70, Tentre Street 1
Stanhope, The Hon. Philip, M.P., 3, Carlton Gardens, London, S.W. 6
Stanworth, Smith, 18, Westgate ... 1
Stanworth, William, 35, Howsin Street 1
Steer, Charles, Clifton, Bristol 1
Strange, Alfred, J.P., Greenfield House 1
Stroyan, Mrs., Brunshaw Road 1
Stuttard, E., Mason's Arms ... 1

Stuttard, Luther, 57, Burns Street 1
Sutcliffe, David, Daisy Cottage ... 1
Sutcliffe, James, Bull Hotel... 1
Sutcliffe, John, 94, Manchester Road 1
Sutcliffe, Robert, 21, Market Street 1
Suthers, A., Public Baths 1

Tanner, W. H., 25, Charlotte Street 1
Tattersall, Arthur, *Independent Press*, Cambridge ... 1
Tattersall, J. F., Bickley, Kent 3
Tattersall, Martin, Colne Road 2
Taylor, Tom, 12, Hebrew Road 1
Thompson, James, 328, Padiham Road 1
Thompson, James W., J.P., Oak Bank ... 1
Thompson, William, Park Side 1
Thornber, Councillor Caleb, 38, Colne Road 3
Thornber, Sharp, Green Hill Terrace... ... 1
Thornber, Alderman T., J.P., The Hollins... 6
Thornton, J., J.P., The Poplars 2
Thornton, Joseph, Temperance Hotel, Bridge Street 1
Thorp, Thomas, Manchester Road 1
Thursby, Sir John Hardy, Bart., Ormerod House 1
Thursby, J. O. S., J.P., Bank Hall 1

Vann, Joseph, 140, Abel Street 1
Varley, Henry, Manchester Road... 1

Waddington, J. C., The Ridge 1
Waddington, Thomas, 9, Albion Terrace 1
Waddington, W. Angelo, Richmond Lodge, Bowdon 6
Walmsley, George, J.P., Tarleton House 6
Walton, Robert, 66, Rectory Road 1
Ward, J. Langfield, M.A., Manchester Road 4
Watson, A. A., L.R.C.P., Holme View ... 1
Watson, J., 74, Railway Street, Nelson 1
Watson, Lawrence, C.C., 4, Park Road, Middlesborough 2
West, Councillor John, Carlton House 1
Whittaker, Dis. Coun. Henry, Hibson Road, Nelson 1
Whittaker, John, J.P., The Woodlands, Nelson .. 12
Whittaker, William, 25, Knightsbridge Grove 1
Wild, Robert, 38, Standish Street ... 1
Wilkinson, Tattersall, Clough Croft Farm 1
Williams, John, 357, Padiham Road ... 1
Witham, Councillor William, J.P., Rockwood 1
Wood, Thomas, 114, Whalley Road, Accrington 1
Woodhouse, Lister, Town Hall, Birkenhead 1

Yates, John, 132, Accrington Road 1

www.ingramcontent.com/pod-product-compliance
Lightning Source LLC
Chambersburg PA
CBHW031427230426
43668CB00007B/463